It's Still Relative

The Word of God for Today's World

Anita Wamble

PublishAmerica
Baltimore

First printing

At the specific preference of the author, PublishAmerica allowed this work to remain exactly as the author intended, verbatim, without editorial input.

All scripture quotes are from the New International Version, (NIV) unless otherwise noted.

ISBN: 1-4137-9219-7
PUBLISHED BY PUBLISHAMERICA, LLLP
www.publishamerica.com
Baltimore

Printed in the United States of America

Dedication

To my dad, James Patterson, yours are the broad shoulders on which I stand and to my father-in-law Dorn Wamble, your never-say-quit attitude rubbed off on me. I love you both.

To my husband Marvin, I still wouldn't want to take this life journey without you by my side.

Acknowledgements

All praise to God the Father, God the Son and God the Holy Spirit.

To my family, Marvin, Julian, Jenise, Alicia, Jayvious, Deniece, Kim – yes, I can watch a WHOLE movie with you now.

Dad and Edna – Every parent should take a note from you parenting book; love your children enough to raise them. All those life lessons you taught me, all those Sunday school and children's church classes you made me sit through have truly guided me throughout this process. Thanks for being my parents and not my friends.

Naomi, Analissa, Aaron and Rena – everyday of this project I thought about you guys and how much you all mean to me. It's great to have brothers and sisters who can be inspirations 3,000 miles away.

Granddaddy and Grand mommy – Ever time I thought about giving up three things you use to say came to mind. Never give up. Never give in. And if you fall down, take a nap and get up fresh for the battle.

Rev. Conrad and Rev. Dr. Diana Parker – No one could ask for better spiritual leaders. Thanks for coming down my street, pulling into my garage and preaching the truth I needed to hear, even if I walked away limping.

To my Sunday school class – Thank you for making me accountable and keeping me on target. May God continue to bless each of you richly.

Contents

Allowing for Growth

Ephesians 4:13 "Until we all reach unity in the faith and in the knowledge of the Son of God and become mature, attaining to the whole measure of the fullness of Christ. "

I can still remember the first time my mother let me walk to the corner store by myself. Walking to the and from the store with my Mom was something I did almost everyday. Then, one day when I asked if we could go, she said "I'm not going to go but you can go by yourself, I think you're old enough now." Then of course she set down all the rules: look both ways before you cross the street, don't talk to anyone, don't get in the car with anyone and most of all, go to the store and come right back.

Oh, I can't tell you how I felt as I walked down the street on my own to go a whole TWO BLOCKS. It felt like freedom, like I was such a big girl and could be trusted to do what my Mom wanted me to do, but I was also a little scared. This was the first time, and what if I did something wrong or what if someone wanted to harm me? But I would not let a little fear stop me from being a big girl. When I got home it was the first time in my life I heard the word maturity. My Mom said to me, "When I let you do things like this, I'm testing your maturity. I want to see how much you've grown up and I can tell that by how well you follow my instructions."

I was on my way into work this morning and the Lord brought this whole story back to me with a little twist. What if I had told my Mom that I was afraid and didn't want to go by myself? Or, what if I went but hadn't obeyed her directions? If I hadn't gone when I did, my growth/maturity would have been stunted and if I hadn't followed her instructions my life could be very different now.

Would my mother have allowed me to walk five blocks to the store? Probably not, I hadn't proven myself mature enough for that kind of responsibility. Would my mother have allowed me to walk with a friend or to a friend's house nearby? More than likely not, because sometimes, especially when you're immature, your "friends" can be more of a hindrance than help. They can pull you away from doing what you know is right, into doing what they want to do.

God works in our lives this same way. He gives us different tests and challenges to test our maturity, in order to "grow us up." He won't give us a test or challenge if He knows we're not ready for it.

Some of us have been praying for certain gifts, talents, abilities or certain material things and God hasn't given them to us yet. We don't have them because He knows we're not mature enough to handle them in an appropriate way.

We're like a child who is three or four who wants a toy designed for a child six to eight year old. A good parent knows that the toddler can't handle a toy designed for an older child and will not give it to them. The parent understands that the toddler can't truly appreciate the toy because they aren't mature enough to understand nor play with it and get the maximum enjoyment out of the toy.

Instead, the parent would give the toddler an age appropriate toy to play with. One that will help him or her work at the skill level that is correct for their age and maturity level.

Well, God the Father is the ultimate good parent.

God has made very specific request and asks us to follow them. God has asked that we not lie. He has asked that we not gossip. God has asked that we give 1/10 of our earnings to Him, via ministries, on every dollar that comes in our house. Do we do the things we know God has asked us to do? He asks that we separate ourselves from those who are in the Body of Christ, but are not living for Christ. Do we do it? He asks us to love each others as we love ourselves. Do we do it?

God may have asked you to operate in the gift or ministry you already know He's given to you. Do you do it on a consistent basis, or just when it's convenient? Maybe you only operate in your gift, talent, ability or ministry when you're going to be seen. If these motives hit close to home you need to ask yourself, how can God give me some of the things I'm praying for when I don't even do what I know is right with what He's already given me?

11

I was talking to a friend of mine the other day. We'll call her Maggie. She was saying how her grown daughter sometimes acts less mature than her six year old. It seemed that no matter how much Maggie or her husband request their adult daughter ACT like an adult, she just isn't willing.

Maggie lamented, "I don't think she'll ever grow-up. I don't think she'll ever act like a responsible adult. I don't know what we did wrong, but obviously we didn't raise her right or something, so I'm just going to cut her off and see how she does. At some point, she's got to stand on her own."

As Maggie and I were talking, a thought struck me deep in my spirit. How many times has God said of me, "I don't think Anita will ever grow-up in this area or that area of her Christian walk. Every time I put her in a test, she opts out. At some point, I'm just going to have to let her go through to get through. It will be for her own good."

Thankfully, God will never cut any of us off, but He will put in us positions were we'll not be able to opt out of a test. We'll have to mature, one way or another.

Now, if you're like me, you'd rather grow up without being forced into it. You'd rather position yourself to allow God to mature you. But how do you allow God to mature you?

Some of you maybe thinking allowing God to mature me sounds difficult and uncomfortable. I'd be lying to you if I told you that it isn't. Walking in the truth that you know and striving to learn more truth is not an easy task for anyone one, but a necessary task for everyone who wants to grow in

Christ. I'm here to tell you — there is no way around it.

How do you start this process? Start by doing what you know is right. Start following His instructions. It doesn't have to be anything big or expensive, just do what you know you should be doing as a child of the Highest King.

For some of us our lack of maturity in Christ is a matter of bondage like smoking, drinking, overeating, overspending, drugs or sexual immorality. Maybe the manifestation of your maturity is being stumped by a habit like gossiping, not spending time in prayer, not spending time in the Word, or hanging out with the ain'ts instead of the saints.

Ask God for help and move into the maturity of knowing that He cares enough for you that He sent His Son to set you free. *John 8:36* tells us "So if the Son sets you free, you will be free indeed."

Jesus is our Savior—by virtue of that title, He came to save us from the world around us and from our own fleshly desires.

In *Romans 7: 15 – 23* Paul teaches us that sin is STILL living in our lives, even though we've come to Christ. In verse 24 Paul voices his understanding that he is a wretched person, even though he's in Christ and a messenger of the gospel. He is not a wretched person because he doesn't love Jesus. He is a wretched person because even though the Holy Spirit tells him to do what is right, his old nature, which is STILL in him, loves to sin and wants him to do wrong. The tug-of-war is so fierce within, Paul questions who or what could save him from his flesh.

In verse 25 Paul gives us the answer to his and our flesh vs. spirit dilemma. Paul says, "Thank God! It has been done by Jesus Christ our Lord. He has set me free." Since God has no respect of person, if he set Paul free, He has set you and me free as well. WOW!!! Isn't that good news?!?!

God will not love you any less while you allow Him to mature you to a point that your freedom, which WAS won by Christ, is manifested in your current life and situations. No, He won't hold it against you when you fall. He won't laugh at you when you make a mistake and he won't hold it against you when you mistake your will for His voice. On the contrary, He will be there cheering you on to the victory that was won for you by Christ (*I Corinthians 15:57.*)

The Holy Spirit has been given to every born again believer for times such as this. God Himself, through the power of the Holy Spirit will empower you to deny your fleshly desires and walk in complete victory.

You maybe are wondering if all this is really worth your time, effort and energy. You maybe on the verge of deciding that maturing in Christ and living in freedom is too high a price to pay. Maybe you're thinking that you've been where you are spiritually for a long time and you'd just a soon stay there. Okay, but you need to know that God requires that we live our lives up to the level of knowledge we have attained (*Philippians 3:16.*) To fully live up to the level of knowledge we have attained means that we have to fully obey the truth we know.

In my house we have certain rules. Our children

have to make their beds every morning. They have to clean the kitchen when it's their turn. Our son has to empty the garbage twice a week and our daughter has to dust the furniture and vacuum the stairs once a week. These are things they know to do. We don't have tell them or ask them to do these chores. On the appointed days at the appointed times they are to live up to the knowledge that they have to complete these chores.

Our children also know that if they choose not to do their chores at the appointed times and in the correct manner, they will face negative repercussions. You see, my husband and I require obedience from our children for the things they know are right to do and things they know are rightfully theirs to do. All of this is a part of our preparing them for something greater. We're pressing them towards their maturity so they can take on more responsibilities. Not only at home but also out in the world. We, as children of God, need to know that this truth is real for us too.

Being obedient to what we know is good and right in God's sight is essential for our living a mature life in Christ.

One day it just seemed to me that there was so much more to my Christian walk than I was experiencing. So I decided that I would begin to work on areas of my life that I knew needed help from the Holy Ghost. The first place I started working was on my tendency to procrastinate. Things were going well. I was seeing a marked change in how I dealt with deadlines and issues that needed my attention.

After I worked on procrastination for a while and could really see a change in my life, I decided that the next thing I needed to work on was my organizational skills. So I set out to change how I organized things at home. Whew, did it make a difference in my daily life. But, I still felt that something was out of place or missing from my Christian experience.

Then one morning, out of sheer frustration of not understanding why this feeling of incompleteness wouldn't go away, I asked the Lord to lift the burden from me.

"No" was the only answer I got back.

"No," I said, "what do you mean NO? Lord, I've given up procrastination and I'm working on being more organized. I've judged myself, like you told me too and I've identified these two areas that I need to work on. What else do you want?" I've got to tell you, I was none to happy with God's response to my efforts.

"I didn't ask for procrastination nor did I ask for organization," the Lord replied.

"Well no, you didn't." I responded, "I just realized that these are two areas that I need to work on and I'm giving them to you freely." By now, I was getting a little frustrated with God. I really wanted Him to get to the point.

"I don't want them. I want what you don't want to give up."

"Okay Lord, know you've really got me confused. What is it I have that I don't want to let you have?"

"Your tongue," was the only reply from the Father gave. It was the only reply that was needed.

You see, I have been blessed with the gift of words. I can turn a phrase as easy as you turn over in a bed. I can talk in front of five people or 5,000 and it wouldn't phase me in the least bit. And, I have been called to teach and preach the gospel. I've known this since I was in high school, but I've never really wanted to be a preacher or a teacher and I was content to run from what God created me to do for the rest of my life.

In addition to having the gift of words, I had learned that my tongue was the most lethal weapon I had. I could cut someone to little bitty pieces with just a few words. The term I liked to use was "nice nasty." I could tear you to shreds while smiling in your face.

I had taken a gift from God, a gift He had given me to build people up and to bring good news to the lost, the least and the lonely and turned it into a vehicle of venom. God wanted His gift to be used for the purpose that He had ordained it to be used. He was not going to be satisfied with my sacrificing procrastination and organization in place of my obedience to my call to ministry.

In fact, you could liken my sacrificing procrastination and organization to that of the scarifies of lambs, bulls and goats that the priests made in the Old Testament. They simply weren't enough to please God. They were only enough to appease God, and then, for only a short time. That's why Jesus had to die, once for all.

Well, I teach a Sunday school class now and preach whenever anyone asks me too. Was it easy to give my tongue to God? Truthfully, some days are easier than others. My maturity in Christ is tested every day because I still struggle with holding my tongue when I really want to rip somebody's head off.

When I began this journey of giving my tongue back to God, I lost more battles than I won. But, God's grace is sufficient! Now, I win more battles then I lose. God isn't looking for perfection, He's looking for a willing heart and a mind turned towards being obedient to Him.

If you're at the point of feeling like there's something missing from your walk with the Lord, ask Him what's missing. Ask Him what He wants from you. He will give you the wisdom you need to press forward to the full maturity that Jesus' death obtained for you and me (*James 1:5-7.*)

The next time the Father asks you to stretch and do something out of your comfort level—go ahead and do it. Allow Him to bring you into a new level of maturity. It may not feel good at first, you may even be a little scared, but do it any way. Over time, if you continue to be obedient you'll find that your flesh will protest less and less each time you override its desires by being obedient to God.

If you want a real and true example of maturity, look at Christ. "My Father, if it is not possible for this cup to be taken away unless I drink it, may your will be done." In *Matthew 26:42b* Christ was mature enough to suffer for the will of God to be complete. In His humanness, Jesus didn't want to go through the suffering, but in His spirit was willing to submit.

PRAYER:

Lord, you have control of my life. You are the essence of my being, the very depth of who I am, without you I am nothing. I want to allow you to mature me in Your word thereby, maturing me in your ways. I want to know your plans for me. Your plans to prosper me and not to harm me. Your plans to give me hope and a future. In order to know your plans I must mature to a place where I can understand, accept, acknowledge and carry out your plans for my life. I submit to your plans for me. Thank you Lord for thinking enough of me to plan my life to have prosperity and hope in Christ Jesus. Amen.

Grace and peace be unto you from God our Father and the Lord Jesus Christ.

God Works in Strange and Mysterious Ways

Standing atop the slave castle, it was easier to hate then to allow God to minister to my heart. I stood there, wanting to cry, because inhumanity surrounded me. It didn't seem like a likely place for God to take the opportunity to minister to me about His grace and perfect will.

Standing on the roof of Elmina Castle, also known as St. George's Castle, looking over the Atlantic Ocean, wondering how many lives laid in its watery grasp of death, did not seem like the most opportune time or place for God to show me His hand in my life and His great love for me.

In the winter of 2000, I traveled to Ghana West Africa for a cultural heritage journey. It was an opportunity I couldn't pass up. The thought of walking in the land of my great ancestors and seeing what my ancient homeland looked like, captivated my curiosity and spoke to my soul.

I knew that the majority of all slaves that left the African continent and traveled to the Americas and

Europe during the Euro-American slave trades had come through the West African slave castles. Through the *doors of no return*, the slave castle doors—which sit on the pristine watery blue shores of the Atlantic Ocean—Africans were led to awaiting ships and foreign lands. And the *doors of no return* were just that. Once passed through, they never opened again to welcome the soon-to-be slaves back home.

I knew a portion of the hideous history of the slave trades, but I was not prepared for what I saw or heard. I was not prepared to see this blight on world history from God's perspective.

We made our way to the slave castles. The members of our tour chatted as the bus maneuvered through the city streets. I watched the children walk to school in beautiful uniforms. Some uniforms were dark brown with gold shirts, others navy pants, skirts or jumpers with white or baby blue blouses. Despite their clean and pressed appearance, I noticed the children had no books or backpacks. Where were their schoolbooks and satchels?

It finally clicked in my mind; the children had no backpacks, because they had nothing to put in them. They have few if any books at their schools. Most schools do not have desks to speak of and few have chalk, paper or pencils. That's why they ask us to bring notebook paper and pencils, to donate it to local schools.

"Why aren't any older kids going to school?" someone near the back of the bus asked.

"There are no free schools in Ghana like there are in the United States," Phil, our tour guide, from the Ashanti region of Ghana, informed us. "Here, in Ghana, you have to pay for school. Some families can't pay to put their children in school and feed them. So, if a child gets to go to school when they're young, when get old enough they stop going to school and work to help the family. But, a lot of children don't go to school at all."

We were traveling along the coast line and overlooking the ocean. The view was spectacular. Small fishing boats bounced up and down in the dark blue waters. Seemingly gentle white caps rolled towards the shoreline of white sand.

Some fishermen had brought in their catch for the day and they were selling them from boats. Women in brightly colored dresses with children on their hips, backs and beside them were bartering with the fishermen for the catch.

Suddenly, I saw the first castle. Its foundation loomed above the activities below like a sentry standing watch over the lives not consumed centuries ago.

Leaving the bus and walking to the castle was a journey of pure emotion. Lost in my thoughts, I barely noticed the people trying to sell me beads and dresses. I was being called to see, to hear and to experience the hand of God in a place I would have never thought I'd find His will at work.

Our castle tour guide's deep bass voice commanded attention, and with the precision of a surgeon, he began cutting away what we thought about this portion of history and began to press the truth about the past into our current consciousness.

The smells of human desperation still lingered in the rooms were thousand upon thousands of slaves had been stored. The courtyard of rape and despair still had the posts, shackles and chains in place. They were reserved for those prisoners who decided that they were not going to loose their freedom without a fight.

The prison rooms still had the fingernail marks on the walls from captives long ago, and the dungeon of the dead had the bones of its victims embedded in the stone floor.

Above the male prisoner's holding area was a United Methodist Church, which Phil explained was fully operational during the slave trades. I wondered how loud those "good Christians" had to sing songs of praise to the God of all creation in order to drown out the cries and moans of the imprisoned souls below them every Sunday morning.

Then, our tour guide took us on "the last walk." This walk ended at the *doors of no return*. Thousand of African lost their lives in those dungeons, which pales in comparison of the millions that lost their lives during the middle passage.

As I stood on the roof looking out over the waters and tried to wrap my brain around all the emotions I had experience, my Pastor walked up to my husband and I and began to talk about all God had done, even in the midst of the slave trade.

I considered for a moment how special I must be

to God. Through all the lives that were snuffed out during the Euro-American slave trades, God saw fit to bring my ancestors through it all, just so I could be here, and experience this.

Generations of Africans died in those dungeons, in the waters of the Atlantic and during the periods of slavery, reconstruction and Jim Crow. But somehow, God saw fit to watch over me—bringing me to the United States, through slavery and all other obstacles.

My anger abided and while I stood on the roof of the slave castle, I saw the true Sovereignty of God.

Understanding that God can take something as heinous as slavery and make something good come out of it only shows that He is true to His word in *Romans 8:28*, "And we know this, that all things work together for good for those who love the Lord and are called according to His purpose."

We were all born with a purpose. Born with God's will resonating in our very existence and God will not allow anything to thwart His plan. (*Psalm 33:11*.)

Through the blood of Christ, we are all under the authority of the only true and living God, who went to extraordinary lengths to make sure that everyone of us got here, to this appointed place, at this appointed time, to fulfill our God-given purpose (*Ephesians 1: 11 – 14.*)

Whether God saw us or our ancestors through a slave ship from Africa, a passenger ship from Europe or a makeship boat from Haiti we can all lift our voices and thank God for His wisdom and unfathomable love for all His children (*Isaiah 54:10.*)

God works in strange and mysterious ways, His wonders to perform.

PRAYER:

Father God, thank you for thinking enough of me to make sure I get to the places you've appointed for me here on earth, as you have already ordained my paths in the heavenly realm. Thank you for thinking so much of me that you designed my past to give me everything I need in the way of character building, moral soundness and ethical standards—for the destiny you're taking me to; through the power of the Holy Spirit that is active in me.

Thank you for calling me your child, a joint heir with your only begotten son Christ Jesus and a co-worker with you.

Father, when I am in doubt about my current situations and circumstances please remind me that your plans for me are perfect, even though I'm not perfect and I live in an imperfect world.

When my days seem hazy and uncertain, remind me that your word is my guiding light and nothing or any one can change the plans you have for me. When fear and doubt creep into my heart and mind and try to paralyze me from carrying out your commands for my life, remind me that I have all authority in the earth. Because of the gift of salvation you've given me, I am more than a conquer through Christ Jesus.

Hallelujah, thank you Lord God. In Jesus name I pray. Amen.

He Will Answer – Part I
Just Keep Asking

Matthew 7:7 - 8 (Amplified) "Keep on asking and it will be given you, keep on seeking and you will find, keep on knocking (reverently) and (the door) will be opened to you. For everyone who keeps on asking, receives, and he who keeps on seeking finds, and to him who keeps on knocking, (the door) will be opened. "

If you asked my earthly father why he seems to favor me over my brother and sisters, he would tell you that he doesn't favor me. And that's the truth. My earthly father loves all five of his children equally. He just always gives me everything I ask for because, as he says, "I worry him down."

When I ask my earthly father for something, I don't just ask once. I ask until he gives me what I want or tells me he absolutely won't give it to me. When my earthly father says, "I'll see about it" or

"Let me think about it," to me that just means to continue to ask until I get a firm yes or no.

And when he says yes, my next question is when? Not that I don't trust my earthly father, but I need to know when I can expect the thing I'm asking for, so I can prepare to receive it.

In the above scripture, God tell us to ask and keep on asking; don't stop seeking Him and don't stop knocking at His kingdom's doors. "Keep on," our heavenly Father exhorts us, "don't stop until I've given you an answer. My answer may be yes, no or maybe, but keep asking until I give you an answer."

How many times have we given up asking for something and not waited for the answer? How many times have we simply walked away from something that we truly wanted or needed to have in our lives, because God didn't answer in the time frame that we desired? How many times have we gone without or gone with less, because we neglected to continue to ask God for what we needed?

Am I telling you to beg God? No, I'm saying that God hears the prayers of His children and more than any earthly father, He wants to give us the desires of our hearts here on earth.

In *Philippians 4:6 - 7* Paul tells us not to be anxious or worried about anything, but to pray and "present" our supplications or "specific request" to God. Paul doesn't say present them once or twice, but "do not be anxious about anything;" which means anything that would make you anxious or worried should be presented to God as an issue in your life that is causing you anxiety. And, after you present the difficulty to Him, rest in His peace, which is a promise from God.

If we give Him our worries, cares, anxieties and heartache, He is faithful to take them and in exchange He will give us peace, which transcends or surpasses or is far above our understanding. This peace will also guard our hearts and minds, (*Psalms 55:22*.)

How can God's peace guard our hearts and minds? God said that He would keep us in perfect peace if we keep our minds stayed on Him (*Isaiah 26:3*.) Real peace of mind can only come from God. There are no drugs—legal or illegal—that can give you real peace of mind. You maybe okay while you're on them, but stop taking them for a while and you'll find that worry and anxiety are waiting for their opportunity to come in and ride rough-shot over your life and make you miserable.

I have a good friend who suffers with anxiety. Everything is a reason to be afraid. Everything is a reason to worry. One day I asked her if she had prayed about something and she said, 'Yes, I've prayed about it, but it didn't do any good. I still have the problem and it's not going away until I do something about it.' When I asked her what she could do that God couldn't do, she looked and me and stuttered something about where is God when you need Him.

God is the only one who knows the true meaning of "perfect timing." We know when we want something to happen. We know when we think we need something to go through, but God knows perfection of time. He is the reason *Ecclesiastes 3:11a* was written, "He has made everything beautiful in its time." Because God knows what His will is for us, God is the only one who can say when the time is right for Him to manifest what we need or what we're asking Him to do.

If my friend had turned over her anxiety to the Lord, and trusted Him to handle every problem that was confronting her, she wouldn't have been so riddled with depression and would have been able to enjoy her life to a greater fullness.

I remember once, when my husband and I were in financial difficulty. I hated to hear the phone ring, because I knew it was a bill collector. I dreaded going to the mail box because it was filled with threatening letters. I was worried all the time about how we were going to make ends meet. Then my husband and I started arguing, something we don't normally do. I was edgy, jumpy and irritable all the time.

I started selling cosmetics as a second job for extra money. The selling brought in the wanted dollars, but left zero family time. Not being able to spend time with my young son because I was out peddling cosmetics just added to my stress. I asked the Lord to take away all the anxiety, stress and worry. I prayed that He would take care of the bills that were haunting us and make everything better again.

The Lord gently directed me to *Matthew 6:25-34*, but the verses that really hit me were *32 and 33*: "For the pagan runs after these things, and your heavenly Father knows that you need them. But seek first his kingdom and his righteousness, and all these things will be given you as well."

I remember being so discouraged after I read this the first time, but after reading it for about the 30th time, it suddenly made all the sense in the world.

God was trying to tell me that He knew my family needed to get out of debt. He knew that my husband and I were worrying ourselves to death over our finances and daily burdens, but He wanted us to trust Him enough to seek Him and His kingdom first.

See, by seeking His kingdom first, you can't dwell on problems. You are so busy trying to fulfill you destiny in Christ that you don't have time to dwell on the problems or burdens that have presented themselves to you. And, while you're seeking God's kingdom for you, you're out of God's way.

God doesn't need a middle man (you and me) to get in His way while He's working things out for our good.

Let me ask you a question: If you're taking test and you run into a questions that you don't know the answer to, do you A) stay on that question and eat up your test time trying to figure it out OR B) do you turn your attention to the other questions on the page and complete what you can? Good test takers will tell you that you turn away from the questions that are giving you problems and complete as many questions as you can during the test period. If you have time, you can return to questions that gave you a problem and you may even find that you have a new perspective on the questions and can now answer them.

That's how seeking the Kingdom of God works. Rather than wasting your time, efforts and energy trying figure out what you should do about something that's worrying you and causing you discomfort—turn your mind to doing what God has directed you to do. Not only will it take your mind off your problems, you will be in a position of obedience to God and obedience brings about blessings (*II Corinthians 9:8.*)

Believe and have faith that God is not a man that He should lie or a son of man that He should change His mind. He's told us that He hears our prayers, and He does. He's told us that if we pray believing we will receive it, we already have. He's told us that nothing is impossible for us, if we do it through Christ Jesus.

So, ask and keep on asking. Seek and keep on seeking, knock and keep on knocking until God gives you His answer. Then, have the courage and the wisdom to follow the path where the answer takes you. I can assure you, it's a trip you won't want to miss.

PRAYER:

Holy God, it is my sincere desire to become mature in my walk with you. To become all that you have called me to be and to watch as you fulfill ever promise you have for me. I will not allow the fear of what other may think or what I have or have not done stop me from growing in you and asking you for what is rightfully mine.

Lord, keep me from the pride of this life and the lust of what I see, hear and feel. Do not allow me to fall into the trap of pride. Keep me ever mindful of how much I need you. All the glory for anything that goes on in my life I give to you and you alone Lord, I don't want it nor do I seek it, but it is for you that I live and by you that I have my being; therefore all glory and honor that comes to me is due to you.

I will always, by prayer and specific request, let everything I need be known unto you and I will allow patience and perseverance to have their perfect work. I will not move without hearing from you, because only you know how, when and what way I'm to go.

I rest, rely and recline my whole self on you, knowing that you not only care for me, but can take care of every need I have.

In Jesus name I pray, Amen.

He Will Answer – Part II

You Better Recognize

Mathew. 8:5 - When Jesus had entered Capernaum, a centurion came to him, asking for help.

The Dilemma –

"Hey, did you have any homework tonight?" I asked my daughter. This was my usual nightly question to her when I pick her up from aftercare.

"Yes, but I didn't finish it."

She didn't finish it? I thought, *now that's a surprise.* My daughter's aftercare takes the kids to the library every day for the expressed purpose of doing their homework. My daughter is an "A" student and normally finishes her homework without any problems.

"Well, what's up? Why didn't you finish it?" I asked.

"I didn't understand my math." Came a small voice reply from the backseat.

"What? You didn't understand your math?"

My daughter, who is one of the most boisterous children you'll ever meet, was obviously having problems admitting that she was having difficulty in school. Her voice was almost a whine and sounded close to tears, "We're doing division and I don't understand it. I don't have all my times table memorized and I don't get it."

"Okay," I replied, "we'll work on it when we get home and I'll help you, alright?"

"Okay. Thanks Mom," and then the backseat sprang to life. My daughter chatted all the way home. It was as if a heavy burden was lifted off her shoulders.

At home, we went over the homework and her multiplication tables and as we did, I remembered having great difficulty with multiplication when I was her age and needing some extra help. As we finished up, I gave her a promise that we would work on her multiplication tables every night until she had them down. She smiled her normal bright smile, thanked me, and then bounced off to practice piano—something she normally hates to do!

As I watched her, the Lord simply spoke to my heart and said, "The problem wasn't her multiplication tables, it was asking for help."

Ah, how I understand that problem. Living in a society that tell us that we should "pull ourselves up by our own boot straps," and "make something out of yourselves for yourselves, by yourselves" we— even Christians, often find it hard to ask for help or to admit that we are in need of something that we can not supply for ourselves. Sometimes, we even find it difficult to go to our Heavenly Father and ask for His help, His grace and His mercy.

The Problem –
This world system is built on pride. Satan was kicked out of heaven because of his pride (*Ezekiel 28:16 – 17,*) and this world order follows him.

God hates pride. Pride will keep us from asking God for the help we need and will lead us down a path of destruction. Pride will cause us to disobey God's commands and His will, in order to fulfill our own lusts and desires. But we need to be mindful that God deals harshly with those who are prideful and haughty in spirit, (*Proverbs 16:5, 18, 10:4 and Isaiah 13:11.*)

King Nebuchadnezzar is a prime example of someone with an overheated pride. But after God caused him to lose his mind and spend seven years thinking he was a wild animal, King Nebuchadnezzar was quick to give glory and honor to God, and recognized His ability to humble those who walk in pride, once he regained his right mind, (*Daniel 4:37.*)

God loves those who are humble in spirit and He gives them grace. God is well pleased with His children who are willing to live in harmony with one another and willing to associate with all kinds of people, even those some might think are "lower class" than you. God will honor a man or woman who is humble in heart, willing to humble themselves before the Lord and are not conceited, (*Proverbs 3:34, 18:12 and Romans 12:16.*)

Our heavenly Father doesn't want us to be ensnared by the same trap that the devil fell into, the trap of pride. Pride is what caused Lucifer to think he could overthrow God, (*Ezekiel 28:17.*) Pride of life will make you want "things" here on earth more than you want spiritual or heavenly things, which will cause you to take you're focus off God and put it on the earthly "things" you want.

Pride will make you believe that you don't need God or that God isn't interested in helping you so you've got to do it yourself. Pride will make you think you can do it all on your own.

You may say you would never consider anything like overthrowing God. You may say that you love God too much for that. But, if you make decisions without consulting the Word of God or without praying about the situation and waiting for an answer from God, you have just acted out of pride.

God shouldn't just "figure into the equation," God *is* the equation. Everything we do in our lives should be to glorify and honor Him.

The Remedy –

There are several truths that we as Christians have to come to believe and stand on by faith:

God is the answer to all our questions and problems. *Jeremiah 10:12* states that God created the world by His wisdom. If that's the case, then what doesn't God know? What can't God answer? What question or problem could you possibly have that would stump God or cause Him to be confused? God's wisdom is wise enough to create the world, to set the standards of morality and ethics.

God has only the best intention toward us. Sometimes to get the best to us or out of us, God has to discipline or correct us. We are His children and as any good parent knows, you can't spear the rod or you'll spoil the child. And while those processes are not enjoyable ones, they are necessary for our growth and development. Father knows best.

God wants to answer every need in our lives through Christ Jesus. Any answer we get to a problem, situation or circumstance that does not put Jesus in the forefront, is the wrong answer. Any answer that includes our compromising our position as children of God is an ungodly answer. God does not need you to lie, cheat or steal to get you to the place where He's purposed you will be in your earthly life. Every answer you get that's from God will come in line with the Word of God, which is Jesus Christ Himself.

In *Matthew 8*, the centurion recognized four things. First, he recognized that he needed help. Second, he recognized who could help him. Third, he recognized that he was unworthy of the help he was about to request and fourth, he recognized the authority of the One he was going to get the help from.

When the centurion recongized that he had exhausted all that he could do and he needed someone with more knowledge, power and authority then he had to solve his problem, be began to peruse the One who represented his solution. When Jesus entered Capernaum the centurion knew about it and went to where Jesus was, and he went for a specific reason—to ask for help.

Let me give you a little insight into the centurion. According to Roman custom, he would have been chosen from among Romans who were stable and reliable and who had demonstrated their courage and maturity. He would have been a well respected individual and because his wages were raised by local taxation, his salary would have been considered "a good one." He was a noncommissioned officer in the world's most feared army of the time, with the responsibility of 100 men under his command. This man was no two-bit nobody. He was someone mighty, who had power and authority in his own right.

But, in spite of all that he may have been or had, the centurion KNEW he needed help, and he humbled himself to a Jew in front of everyone. You see, the Jews were in occupied territory. They didn't run anything and couldn't do anything without the approval of the Roman government, but this officer of the Roman army submitted to the authority he saw in Jesus.

He was in no position to pull rank. He may have been in charge of 100 soldiers, but his rank and title was of no use to him in his current circumstance.

Some of us need to take note of these facts, because we need to understand that our position in life; not our titles, our wealth nor our prosperity negate our need to be humble before God and man.

Since the centurion was a man of means, he had probably done all he could for his servant. I'm sure, even without the Bible specifically saying it, that the centurion had called in doctors to see about his servant. But obviously, the doctors couldn't help so the centurion starting looking for someone who could.

Just like today, the centurion could have used spiritual mediums the equivalent of our modern day psychics. He could have gone to someone who worked in witchcraft or someone who concocted potions with roots (what we call a root doctor.) And maybe he had already gone to them. But they didn't have the authority to do what he needed done.

So the centurion went to the man he had obviously heard about. In verse 9 the centurion reveals why he went to Jesus. It was through his faith; the centurion understood Jesus' power to heal his servant. In other words, he recognized Jesus had authority over the disease in his servant's body and so could command it to be moved. **Read Verse 9.**

We too need to recognize Jesus' authority over every problem in our life. What can't Jesus do? Is He not Jehovah-Rapha, our healer thereby stating that he has authority over diseases and infirmities?

Is He not Jehovah-Elohim, our strong one, the One we can run to in times of distress? Is He not our Yahweh, the One who is, the One who can be what we need Him to be, when we need Him to be it, for as long as we need Him to be it? YOU BETTER RECOGNIZE WHO HAS THE AUTHORITY AND WHO YOU NEED TO ASK FOR HELP!

You may say if authority, dominion and power all come from God, and authority, dominion and power all come to us as born-again believers by the Holy Spirit, and authority, dominion and power have all been made available to us, by our accepting of

Jesus Christ as our savior; then why do we need to ask for what is rightfully ours?

You need to ask out of humility. You need to acknowledge your need for God. You need to make sure you understand that everything you do, everything you've become and everything you have, is only because God has given you the ability to do it, become it and get it, (*Deut 8:17-18.*)

Recognize Him for who He is and He'll give you the desires of your heart.

PRAYER:

Heavenly Father, I've come to ask you to forgive me for not making you the center of all the decisions I make. I ask that you forgive me for not asking for your help more often, but instead relying on earthly measures like credit cards and unbiblical based self-help books and talk shows.

I declare that you are the only wise God both now and forever more. I declare that you are the only God and that you are full of wisdom, power and You give me sound answers for the questions, situations and circumstances of my life. It is only because of your grace and your mercy that I am able to stand in confidence, soundness of mind and wholeness of spirit. Guide my heart and mind from pride in myself, to allowing me to give all glory and honor to you.

In Jesus name I pray, amen.

It's a Virus and It Spreads

I John 3: 4 – 10 "Everyone who sins breaks the law; in fact, sin is lawlessness. But you know that He appeared so that He might take away our sins. And in Him is no sin. No one who lives in Him keeps on sinning. No one who continues to sin has either seen him or known him. Dear children, do not let anyone lead you astray. He who does what is right is righteous, just as he is righteous. He who does what is sinful is of the devil, because the devil has been sinning from the beginning. The reason the Son of God appeared was to destroy the devil's work. No one who is born of God will continue to sin, because God's seed remains in him; he cannot go on sinning, because he has been born of God. This is how we know who the children of God are and who the children of the devil are: Anyone who does not do what is right is not a child of God; nor is anyone who does not love his brother."

I have several computers at my disposal. I have the one at home, one in my office plus I can always use my husband's. All three of the systems have different kinds of software programs installed, but all the systems are window based. So, all the computers operate pretty much the same with just a few adjustments for the new program packages.

One day I was working on my system at home and received an e-mail from an old friend. When I opened the email, it was one of those chain emails, so I deleted. I continued with my work but my system wasn't responding the way it should. Things just weren't acting right.

At first, it was small things so I chalked them up to a computer glitch. But then, the "things" became more noticeable. My sound system started to fade, my computer started freezing up and my programs don't work as fast and then some of them stopped working altogether.

I checked my configurations; made sure everything's set up correctly. Then I checked my connections, to make sure all my apparatus were hooked up right. The system was acting as if it had a mind of its own and it was running amuck. No matter what I did it wouldn't respond appropriately. Then finally, it dawned on me that I had contracted a virus. I had to shut my system down manual. See, no matter how bad this virus was I still had the power to turn my system off.

Getting rid of this virus was a long and drawn out process!!!

I had to fight with my computer to try to get it to work well enough for me to down load new virus protection that would remove the virus from my system and restore my computer to its normal operation. The virus was trying to stop me from loading the remedy, so I had to fight to regain control over my system from this unwanted visitor. Some three or four hours later, the virus was gone and my system was fully operational again.

A virus will destroy files, corrupt documents and ruin the interface the computer has with other equipment, like printers, copiers and scanners. There is not a computer system in the world designed to have a virus running at the same time the system is suppose to be fully operational.

The next day, I received a message from one of my former bosses saying that I had sent him the virus. I found out that not only did my former boss get the virus, but EVERYONE in my contact list. I have friends, relatives, business associates and clients in my contact list. Well over 250 people and all they were infected by a virus that touched my computer system for what seemed to be a very short period of time.

And yes, the computer in my office and my husband's computer were adversely affected by the virus, even though I wasn't on them at the time of the contamination. My office computer and my husband's computer are connected to my home computer because the email addresses of each are in my contact list.

Sin in the life of a Christian is just like the virus that infected my computer. It will destroy the renewal of your mind, corrupt your morals and ethics and ruin your relationship and fellowship with the Father, other Saints, your spouse, your children and other friends and family members.

One "small" sin, left unchecked will cause your walk with Christ to fall into a position of not being fully functional. Sin will cause you to struggle to do the things you know you should do as a child of the Most High God. Sin left to grow and flourish will cause you to loss connection with the Holy Spirit, the Son and the Father because sin runs interference and it doesn't want you to remedy the problem. Our flesh likes the sin. Our spirit is grieved when we sin.

How can we tell if "certain things" in our lives are sins? We can ask you just a couple of questions; am I operating outside of Gods' will and independent of Him? Is "it" contrary to the character of God? And, does "it" glorify God through Christ?

When we operate outside and independent of God we are operating by the pride of life, the lust of the eye and the boasting of what we have or what we do, which doesn't come from the Lord but from the world and Satan who is the prince of this world. We need to remember that this world system and Satan have been put on notice of their eternal condemnation and judgment, (*I John 2:15 – 17; John 12:31 and John 16:11.*)

Remember, we are in the world but not of the world. We are to renew our minds and put them on things above and not on earthly things. We should be more concerned about what God thinks of us then of what other people think of us. We should strive to reflect the character of God in everything we do. Showing the love of God through our lives is what gives God glory and it's what draws the spiritually lost to us so we can tell them about Christ, (*Colossians 3:2; Romans 12:2; John 12:43; John 15:19; Ephesians 5:2 and John 17:1.*)

James 4:4 gives a clear point of view about Christian who still live in carnality and love the world more than God—"You adulterous people, don't you know that friendship with the world is hatred towards God? Anyone who chooses to be a friend of the world becomes an enemy of God."

Dealing with sin is a lot like dealing with a virus on a computer. First, you realize something's wrong and decided you want to do something about it.

There are only a few ways you can get a virus: 1. No anti-virus protection on your system, 2. Outdated anti-virus protection on your system. 3. Have a virus so deceptive that it can worm its way past your protection.

Once you realize that you have a virus, you have to purge it from your system or it can and will corrupt and ruin everything that you've worked so hard on, or it can crash your hard-drive altogether. Even worse, the virus may worm itself into your address book and send itself out to all your friends and family and poison their systems as well. The effects of a virus are far reaching and damaging.

So it is with sin. When you call yourself a dedicated Christian, one who purposes to live an upright and holy life before God, you will have a hard time, if not an impossible time, living in habitual sin.

Habitual sin, that's the kind of sin that John is talking about in *I John 3:4*. Yes, we all sin and come short of the glory of God. And yes, we all need new grace and new mercy every day. But that kind of unconscious sin is not what John is talking about.

John is talking about the kind of sin that we live in day after day. Knowing it's a sin but refusing to allow God to deal with it, or us in an appropriate way. It's wrong and we know it, but we refuse to come out of it.

It's wrong to cheat on your lawfully-wed husband or wife, but you do it anyway. It's wrong to physically, mentally or emotionally abuse your husband or wife, but you do it anyway. It's wrong to neglect your children, but you do it anyway. It's wrong to be a workaholic, but you do it anyway. It's wrong to lie, but you do it anyway. It's wrong to be hateful, but you do it anyway. It's wrong to gossip, but you do it anyway. It's wrong to eat your way into bad health, but you do it anyway. It's wrong to set up fantasy worlds in your mind so that you don't have to deal with the realities of your own life, but you do it anyway. It's wrong to create division in the church, but you do it anyway. It's wrong to stand behind tradition, when God is leading another direction, but you do it anyway. **That's the kind of sin John's talking about.**

One habitual sin left in our lives, can worm its way into every facet of our life. And just like the computer virus, it can destroy all that you have worked for in your spiritual life. At first, it's just little things. You're not praying as much as you use too. You're not in the Word as much as you were.

You're not hanging out around the saints any more. You stop coming to church on a regular basis.

The next thing you know, that "thing," whatever it is that you thought you were delivered from, raises its ugly head and you heed its call. Then you are pulled and drawn away from Christ, by your own lust and the desire of your flesh. Then the next "thing" crops up, and you give in. This time it's easier than the last time. And on and on the cycle goes and before you know it, every facet of your life has been corrupted by the virus of just one habitual sin that you allowed to stay active in your life.

But that's not all. Your children, your spouse, your spiritually carnal neighbor and that new Christian that just joined the church have been watching you. They want to know what a real Christian looks like. They know you're one, because you go to church. They know you're one because you know a couple of Bible scriptures. They know you're one, because you told them. So, they can live like you and be saved too, right?

Wrong, because when we live like this, we can't say like Paul, "Follow me as I follow Christ," (*I Corinthians 11:1*,) because you're not following Christ. You're following your instincts. You're following your intuition. You're following the desires of your heart and the lust of your eye. That's not following Christ. But now, because they're watching you, they think they can live like you and be an effective Christian. And the virus of habitual sin has now spread.

But just like a computer virus has only a few ways of infecting a computer, the virus of habitual sin has only a few ways of getting into our lives and infecting us. 1. We have no anti-virus protection, meaning we aren't in the Word. We don't pray and we don't hang out with the saints. 2. We do pray, but it's only in passing and when we think about it, we only know the Lord's Prayer, the 23rd Psalm and one of the nine beatitudes. Therefore, our anti-virus protection is out of date and can't ward off the attacks of the enemy. 3. You missed seeing the temptation for what it was and it wormed its way in, before you realized what you were really up against.

But just like a computer, we Christians have a sin virus remedy. They are called repentance and the Holy Spirit. When the Holy Spirit detects a sin virus in God's temple, He sends out an interceptor and He, the Holy Spirit, will quarantine the virus. Now, this is where we come in. We have the ability to grieve the Holy Spirit. Quench His authority in our lives, and loose the virus and live out the sin that the virus brings.

Or, we can repent of our sins and allow the Holy Spirit to have His perfect work in our lives. If we allow the Holy Spirit to have the authority over our lives that is rightfully His, then He will rebuke the virus and drive it out. But we have to resist the sinful nature that is craving to carry out the sin that the virus brings.

We are all tempted by our enemy Satan, and our flesh to sin. If you choose to habitually live in and carry out sin, you need to check and see if you ever accepted Christ as Savior and Lord. (*Galatians5:19 – 21*.) If you're in a battle and the sin virus is trying to get though your defenses, remember; the temptation can only come into your life if YOU let it in, otherwise the Holy Spirit will keep it at bay, (*James 1: 13 – 15.*)

So what will you choose to be—a Saint that allows the Holy Spirit to boot out the virus of this world order or will you choose to be an Ain't, and allow the viruses of this world to rule your life? The choice is yours.

PRAYER:

Father God, I come before you repenting of my sins. Those known and unknown. I purpose to live my life for Your glory. Search me Lord, for you know me completely. Cleans me Lord, so that I may be a usefully vessel. A vessel for noble purposes. Bring my will in line with your will for me and cause my heart to turn completely to you. Father, if there is anything in me that is not like you begin the process of removing it so that I may reflect your Son Jesus in everything I do and in every word I say. Father, from this day forward let there be a change in me that brings glory and honor to you. In Jesus name I pray, amen.

May God Bless You.

Letting Go - Part I
Let His-story Speak for Itself
John 21

In a recent study by the Department of Justice, it is estimated that 67.5% of individuals convicted and incarcerated for a crime will return to prison within three years from the time they are released back into the free world.

One of the biggest problems for repeat offenders is they return to the same environment they were in before they were incarcerated initially and begin to do the same things that put them in jail or prison in the first place.

As one ex-offender put it, "Sometimes, you just don't know what to do. You know you need to do something, but you don't know what "it" is. You don't know where to begin, but you know you have to start somewhere, so you start from where you know."

Can you imagine what the disciples must have felt like after they lost Jesus as a human leader? They knew they needed to do something, but they didn't know what "it" was that they needed to do. The Holy Spirit hadn't come upon them yet, so they hadn't received power and the fact that they went into hiding after Jesus' crucifixion showed that they, even Peter, were a scary bunch of men.

They knew they needed to do something, but they didn't know what and they didn't know where to begin. For the last three and a half years they had been following Jesus, and since He was gone from their physical lives they are not sure what do to.

Even though Jesus had been crucified, died, resurrected, and had visited with the disciples they still didn't know what to do. Jesus had allowed them to walk with Him and learn from Him, but still they didn't know what to do now that He was gone. He had told them over and over again that what was going to happen, but it's obvious from their reaction that they didn't believe Him.

So Peter makes a decision, he's going fishing and some of the other disciples decide to join him. Not fishing men, which is what Jesus called Peter and the other disciples to do, no—they were going to fish for fish. This is what many of them did before they received their call from Jesus.

These men saw Jesus feed the 4,000 and the 5,000 men. Peter, James and John saw Jesus' transfiguration and watched as He raised Jairus' daughter back to life. All the disciples had witnessed Jesus healing the sick, casting out demons and even speaking to the winds and to the waves and making them become peaceful and still. You would think after a history like that, they would continue the ministry Christ trained them for, but they were too much like us.

The disciples found themselves in an uncomfortable situation, much like the ex-convicts we talked about earlier, and the disciples like the convicts decided to go back and do what they had done before. They decided that knowing what Jesus had taught them was not enough to make a difference in their lives.

When we find ourselves in uncomfortable situations, difficult circumstances and tight spots, do we forget what we've been taught by the Word of God? When we are facing a job lost, do we forget all the times the Lord has made a way out of no way and that He has given us strength to make wealth?

When we find ourselves facing financial difficulties, do we forget that all our needs are supplied by His riches in glory, thorough Christ Jesus? Do we forget our His-story with Him? When we can't see how God's going to work it out, do we stop relying on Him and go back to handling things our way?

You see people going back to the very thing that almost destroyed them all the time. Just watch VH-1 or E!. You'll see multi-millionaire television and movies stars and musicians that have battled drugs, alcohol, food and sexual misconduct and immorality that almost killed them. Often, not just once or twice, but many times they battle their inward demons. Each time worse than the previous bout with the addiction. But repeatedly, when things get difficult they return to the same destructive behavior.

They go into high priced rehabilitation centers.

Their friends confront them at intervention sessions. They may be close to losing their careers or maybe they have a close brush with death, but no matter what, until they learn a different way of dealing with their problems and difficulties, they continue to return to their bad habits.

For some of us, Jesus brought us out of drugs, alcohol and/or food additions or abuses when nothing else could help. He gave some of us enough Christ-esteem so we could come out of sexual immorality long enough to realize there was more to us than what was below our waistline.

For some of us, He brought us out of abusive relationships, whether with parents, siblings or spouses, with our minds still intact. For some of us He broke the yoke of depression, suicide and mental illness. Some of us would be in financial ruin had it not been for His love for us. His turning our hearts to see the truth about who we are in Him, and we're more than what we wear, what kind of car we drive or how big the house is we're living in.

We, unlike many celebrities, have found the real meaning of peace. Our roads to recovery may not be easy, but God is with us every step. Coaching us along. Encouraging us with His word and sending other people to encourage us as we walked out of the darkness that held us captive and into the marvelous light of His Son, Jesus Christ.

We've experienced the kind of freedom that only comes by knowing Jesus as Savior. There isn't enough money in the market place to replace the kind of joy and contentment that comes from knowing you left that old you behind and started fresh in Christ.

I don't know what your His-story is with the Lord, but why don't you draw from it when you are required to walk out a difficult task rather than going back to what you were before you knew Christ?

If God made a promise, He is faithful and just to fulfill it, no matter what the circumstances. God is not a respecter of person. If he did it for one person He'll do it for you.

If you're lonely, He promised to be with you always. If you thirsty for something more, He promised to be your living water. If you need a shoulder to cry on, He promised to give you mothers, fathers, brothers and sisters in this life. If you need a financial break-through, He promised to supply all your needs according to His riches in glory through Christ Jesus.

What do you need?

Why am I spelling history His-story? Because our lives are just that, His-story. His-story of God's great love for us. His-story of His ever-presence in our lives. His-story of grace and mercy to a sinful, hateful, evil and perverse people. His-story that was, is and will continue to be, what we can remember and draw from when times aren't what we would like them to be, when life has dealt us blows that send us reeling.

Resting in the truth of what God has already done for you require that you call to your remembrance where you were when God found you.

Don't bring your experiences with God to your remembrance to wallow in the despair of where you were. No, bring them to your remembrance so you can praise God for bringing you out from where you were into newness of life. Don't feel guilty about what you were doing when God reached out for you, but remember the mighty works that God has already done in your life.

You need to remember what God has done so that you can measure it up against what you need Him to do for you now.

Every time you face a problem think about it like this: What's easier? For God to have saved your soul from hell or to meet my need for a new job? For God to have delivered me from self-destructive habits or for Him to pay a bill?

Is it easier for God to erase the pain that plagued your heart for years or for Him to save your marriage? Was it easier for Him to pay for your children's college tuition or get you a new car? What does your His-story tell you?

PRAYER

Lord, I thank you for the His-story I have with you. You have been with me from the beginning. You appointed everything in my life. My birth and all the circumstances surrounding it were appointed by you. My life at every turn has your fingerprints all over it. There is nothing about me that you don't know.

Please Lord, help me to remember my life was set apart by your appointment and by Your will, and everything that you ordained for me shall come to pass. Help me not to view my hardships, trials or tribulations as permanent; thereby causing me to deal with the problem as a permanent fixture in my life. Help me to view the difficulty with a Christ-like understanding and Godly wisdom, recognizing what you have already done for me and stand on the fact that the problem I am now facing will work for my good, because I love the Lord and have been called into your royal order. Jesus is my Lord and the Most High God is my Father, therefore I have no need to worry or fear, for Jesus is my very present help in the time of trouble.

Thank You Lord for helping me to see with spiritual eyes that I do not have to worry about life or body, for you have already prepared a plan to take care of my every need. A plan to prosper me not to hurt me— you are my hope and my future. Thank you Lord for your words of assurance and your acts of loving kindness that you shower on me daily from heaven above. In Jesus name I pray. Amen.

Letting Go – Part II

What We Have Become

I Samuel 16:1 – 13

Out of Someone Else's Normal and Into My Destiny

David was a shepherd boy and in the eyes of his father and his brothers that was all he was ever going to be. When Samuel came looking for the next king of Israel, David wasn't even called to come from the fields to be inspected by Samuel until all his brothers had been rejected by God and God instructed Samuel to ask for him.

Men often judge by what we see and hear. We look at the outward appearance of someone because we can't judge the heart. But the Bible says that God has placed eternity in the heart of men. In other words, God has placed in each of us a yearning and desire to become what God created us to become. He's placed in our innermost person a need to reach the potential of who we are in Christ.

There are times in our lives, just like with David, when people want to pigeonhole us into what they think we should be, how they think we should act and what they think we should look like. But God doesn't put people in little boxes like man does. God does not require that we follow a certain pattern like everyone else. In fact, look around you and you'll see just how much God loves diversity.

There are people of every shape and size. People who are outdoors folks and then others that think you're roughing it if you're not the on concierge level of a hotel. God only requires that we follow the paths that he's laid out of us.

There is a story told of a young man named Ernest Masterson, who wanted to be an architect. He dreamed of designing skyscrapers and business parks in Northern California or maybe New York. He wanted to go to the best architectural college in the United States and set his sights on University of Michigan.

But the men in Ernest's family were blue collar workers. Welders and plumbers were the family's trades. His great-grandfather had been a welder, his grandfather a plumber. His uncles were welders and his Dad was a plumber. All were proud of their legacy and they wanted it to pass down for many generations.

From the time male children in the Masterson family were old enough to know the difference between a blow torch and an elbow joint, they were working side by side with their dads, granddads and uncles learning their trade.

Two of Ernest's brothers, Martin and Dale followed the footsteps of their forefathers. One was a plumber and the other a welder, but his brother

Robert decided that he was going to be an electrician.

No one in the family saw the value of college, in fact the family usually spoke ill of those who obtained a college degree.

The family members couldn't understand why Ernest worked so hard in school to get good grades. Imagine the families shock when Ernest informed them that he was going to take the SAT because he wanted to go to college.

His father reminded him that no one in the Masterson family had gone to college. In fact, college was for soft "delicate" men and the Mastersons' were real men, who worked with their hands and earned a living by the sweat on their brow. Ernest would break the tradition of the family males to become plumbers, welders and now electrician, if he continued to pursue this foolishness of going off to college.

Ernest had been raised to be obedient to his parents, but he felt a stronger pull to pursue something deep inside that could not be fulfilled by sticking with family tradition.

Ernest took the SAT and got descent scores. His counselor helped him fill-out college applications and the necessary paperwork for scholarships and grants.

Knowing that his father would never sign the paperwork, he took it to his mother and asked if she would do sign it for him. Understanding her son needed to be who he was created to be, Vive Masterson signed the paperwork and mailed everything off to the appropriate agencies and college while her husband was at work.

All Ernest's hard work paid off. He won a full scholarship to the University of Oklahoma. It wasn't Michigan, but it would have to do.

Ernest family never approved of his choice to go to college, and vowed they would not help him financially, but when he got tired of trying to be "something he wasn't," he could come home and they would help him find a real job.

Ernest worked everyday for four years in a work study program. Thankfully, the scholarship covered his dorm expenses so he always had someplace to call home while he was in Oklahoma. But he never went home over the holidays or during school breaks. He couldn't afford too and his father wouldn't send for him.

In the summers before his junior and senior years of college, Ernest got a job with a local architectural firm. One of the senior architects was so impressed with his enthusiasm and his willingness to learn, he took Ernest under his wing and taught him about the business of running an architectural firm, as well as the business of design and developing an eye for design and space.

Four years seemed to fly by and before he knew it, Ernest was ready to graduate. He sent his invitations to all his family members, but they refused to attend his graduation. He walked across the stage to the cheers of his friends and the senior architect, who offered Ernest his first job.

Since that time, Ernest has build homes,

skyscrapers and mini-malls all over the country. He has fulfilled the passion and the desire that burned in his heart.

He's even been able to help his family out financially and take care of his ailing Father.

Ernest knew that he was something other than a plumber, a welder or an electrician and he was willing to do whatever it took to become something more than what others saw in him. He wasn't going to let anything; not tradition, not hard-times or disappointment stop him from being all that he was created to become.

Sometimes, we are called out of our current situation and into our destiny like David was, but other times, we've got to walk out our destiny in spite of what other may think or say. We've got to know that if God called us to it, then our gifts will make room for us.

Are you sitting still and allowing your eternity to eat away at your spirit person, causing you discomfort that you can't explain? Are you struggling with knowing you're more than others give you credit for? Or, are you fighting within yourself to move past your fears and reach for the unknown because you know that God has ordained something more for you?

If you answered yes to any of these questions then you need to move into your destiny. Move past your previous defeats and past your failures of yesterday. Move past your fears that are holding you in bondage and past the possibility of rejection. All of these are tricks of the enemy. The devil doesn't want you to reach your destiny because he knows that if you do hundreds, possibility thousands or millions of lives maybe affected by the eternal plan that is in you.

If you're called out like David, then go. But if not, you've got to go anyway, just like Ernest. Neither David nor Ernest had it easy. Both had to scale mountains of obstacles, wade through valleys of doubt and swim through rivers of nay sayers, but in the end, they both became what they were created to be and their respective worlds were better places because of their struggle.

PRAYER:

Heavenly Father, I know that you've bound up eternity in my heart, but I'm not sure what destiny you have for me. I want to fulfill all that you have in store for my life, but I don't know what it is, please show me what it is you want me to do and what purpose I have in life.

Lord, I'm relying on you to bring my eternity into reality as I put you and the Kingdom of God first, knowing that everything I need will be given to me as the needs arise.

I put my hope in you and the Spirit of Christ that lives in me. I am able to do exceeding and abundantly more than I could ever give myself credit for by the power that lives and works in me.

The Word of God that I have hidden in my heart will be a lamp unto my feet and a light unto my path. The Holy Spirit will lead me and guide me into all truth and I will not lean on my own understanding but in all my ways acknowledge you Lord and you will make my crooked paths straight.

You have not given me a spirit of fear, but of love, power and a sound mind—the mind of Christ. Therefore, I am capable of anything, ready for anything and already have prevision for everything that might come against me through Jesus Christ. And I will view myself as you view me, Lord—a great and victorious child of the Most High God. Thank you Father. In Jesus name. Amen.

This story and all its characters are fictitious. Any similarities to actual people are purely coincidental.

Letting Go – Part III
Fighting to Become the Me I Was Meant to Be
John 21

Peter was a trained to be a fisherman. Historically speaking, he had been in training with his father since he was very young. He knew how to bail and cast the nets. He knew how to bring the nets in so no fish would be lost. He knew all the tricks of the trade.

From Matthew to John and even in the letter to the churches, we also find that in addition to being trained in the art of fishing, Peter was bold, loud, zealous, and fearful. If the way got tough, Peter would turn his back on his friends; he'd go into hiding and become a man-pleaser.

We find that Peter sometimes had a hard time fulfilling the life work that had been given to him by Christ rather than doing what the world trained him to do. His quick temper causes him to cut off a soldier's ear when the solider came for Jesus in the Garden of Gethsemane, yet within a few hours, Peter was denying he knew Jesus.

Peter spoke up and rightfully declared that Jesus was the Christ, but not to long after he made that declaration, in fear he was in hiding from the Roman soldiers. If Peter had really believed that Jesus was the Christ and that all the prophecies surrounding the Christ would come to pass, then would he have been so fearful?

Paul had to rebuke Peter in *Galatians 2:11-13*. Paul and the other elders, including Peter, had made an agreement in the book of Acts regarding how they would deal with and treat Gentile Christians. Peter went back on his word because he was afraid of what another group of Jews would say if they saw him eating with the Gentiles. Peter went back to what he was; a frightened man-pleaser, rather than standing up for what he knew was right. He reverted back to what he was in order to fit in and get along. Sound familiar?

At one point or another in our lives, when it's convenient and comfortable, we all go back to what we were, if we haven't resolved to be what Christ has called us to become, (*I King 19:1-9; 1 Sam. 28:8-19; Mat. 12:44-45.*)

Some of us go back to being afraid of what others will think if we do what the Holy Spirit urges us to do. Sometimes we become men-pleasers because we want people to "like us." Sometimes we go back to that boyfriend or that girlfriend, even though we're married, because we "had a hard week and just needed someone to talk to."

Sometimes we go back to that lover, even though we're not married because we don't trust God enough to meet us at our point of need. Sometimes we go back to gossiping because talking about someone else's shortcomings makes us feel better about our own.

Whatever you go back to, just know that God does not allow for folly, foolishness or sin in the name of "previous training."

Once you come to Christ, you are a new creature. Your new training begins, and the Drill Sergeant is the Holy Spirit. You get a new training manual, the Word of God. Old things must be allowed to pass away, so that the new training you have now placed yourself under can take hold and renew your mind.

This is not a volunteer draft option; once you've decided to come to Christ, it's mandatory.

What do you think would have happened to David, and all of Israel, if David hadn't stepped up to the plate against Goliath? What do you think would have happened if he had listened to his brother and went back home to tend to the sheep without first tending to the giant?

How many times do we opt out of God's training plan of our lives because we think it's too hard? How many times are we willing to go back to something that isn't God's desire for us just because it can get us through?

How many times are we willing to listen to other people's opinions of us rather than walk out the path that God has sit before us.

Becoming King was God's plan for David. Not his brothers, his father or any of his uncles. So they didn't understand how God could pick David out of everyone to be the next king., It wasn't their plan. It wasn't their will. It wasn't their desire, it was God's and his is the only one that matters. Not even David's plan for himself matter more than God's plan for him.

So how can someone else tell us what we can or cannot do? How can we allow someone else to place limits on our lives when we serve a limitless God? Why do allow anyone; parents, teachers, spouses, family members or friend to determine our destiny?

They don't know what God has set in your heart. They don't know what you dream of in the quiet time of the early morning hours. They don't see the mental images of your life work in God hands. And, they don't know all that you have become through Christ Jesus. Nothing is impossible with God.

So what will it be? Will we become what other people say we are or what we've been trained to be? Or, will we stand on the new training that comes from our Heavenly Father and reach beyond what we see or what we were and become what He's created us to be?

The choice is yours, but knows this; your stages of blessing depend on your choice.

God blesses those who are obedient and adhere to His commends, precept and laws. Not just the ones in the Word of God, but also the ones He gives you specifically.

If God has told you to start a neighborhood Bible study or to go to work in a school in your community helping to tutor children who have difficulty reading, JUST DO IT, and allow the Lord to bless you.

When God asks us to do something that we can't accomplish in our own strength, don't worry about it. God knew our limitations before He asked. He just wants to know if you love Him enough to obey Him, even through your fears and doubts.

He wants to use these challenges in our lives to show Himself strong and to get the glory out of our lives. Don't forget David and Goliath. David could never have defeated Goliath with his own strength and know how. He wasn't strong enough and he didn't know how.

But, he had enough faith and trusted God to go out and put his self on the line. Through David's experiences with bears and lions, God had taught him to trust Him. So, with a heart full of faith and a pocket full of rocks, David faced what some would think was an insurmountable obstacle and won.

And when he had slain Goliath, he was rewarded with great treasures, the King's daughter as his bride and favor for his family. Obedience will bring about rewards.

God never sets us up for failure only for victory, (*I Corinthians 15:57 – 58.*)

PRAYER

Father, forgive me for allowing myself to grieve the Holy Spirit, which seals my eternal salvation, when I fall back to what I was before you took over my life. Forgive me Father, for allowing my fear of what others may think to stop me from doing what you have anointed me to do. Forgive me Lord, when I am disobedient to the Word for the sake of "getting along."

I know you have not given me the spirit of fear, but of love, of power and a sound self-controlled mind. I know that you have called me out of my life of sin in order that I may be your witness; witness that your never-changing love, can turn a life around.

Uphold me Lord, in your righteous right hand, as I walk out the life you have set before me. Thank You Jesus, for protecting me with your precious blood from the enemy's snares and pitfalls. Under gird me as I walk by faith, in the trustworthiness of your word and not by sight, feelings or emotions.

Father God, cause me to be steadfast and immovable as I allow you, by the power of the Holy Spirit, to tear down the strongholds in my life that would cause me to be disobedient to you. Thank You Lord for the victory! In Jesus' name I pray. Amen.

Little Becomes Much - Part I

The Little I Have Is Yours

II King 4: 1 – 7

Have you ever found yourself in need, but no clear path for getting out of it?

Have you ever read a story of someone else's life and the difficulties they went through, only to come out better in the end than they could have ever imagined?

And after you've read those stories, have you ever thought to yourself, "that could never happen to me. I don't have what it takes."

Well, I'm here to tell you that if you have Jesus Christ as your Savior, you do have what it takes and much more.

Little becomes much when you place it in the Master's hands are words from a song that was written many years ago. The song is entitled "Ordinary People." The problem is that most of us don't place what we have in the Master's hand because we think that we've got to be extra-ordinary people to make a difference, but nothing could be further from the truth.

Paul was an ordinary Jew—persecuting the Christians when God did an extra-ordinary thing and changed his life. Matthew was an ordinary betrayer of his people, by working for the Roman's as a tax-collector, but then he met Jesus and Jesus changed his life. Gideon was an ordinary coward— until the angel of God came to visit him and called him what he had yet to become and empowered him to be extra-ordinary warrior. Mary was an ordinary girl until an angel visited her and she became the mother of an extra-ordinary baby.

All of these people did great things after they had a meeting with an extra-ordinary God.

All of us have gifts, talents and abilities that we perceive as "little" or "ordinary." We belittle or berate our gifts, talents and abilities because we have not placed the same value on them that God has placed on. We don't think our gifts, talents and abilities are worth placing in the Master's hands because in our estimation, they're not much of anything.

We may have tried to walk into our destiny a few times and fallen. We may have told our friends and families what the Lord has placed on our hearts and they discouraged us. We may have decided that we were going to step out on faith and fulfill God's call on our lives, just to be met with rejection.

But no amount of adversity should be viewed as a reason to give up. And no gift that God has placed in us should be left untapped.

For just a moment, let's look at some people in

the Bible who had a problem or two, but were still found fit to serve God:

Moses stuttered and was a murderer. David was too young, his armor didn't fit, he had an affair and put a contract on a man's life. John Mark deserted Paul. Timothy had ulcers. Hosea's wife was a prostitute. Amos' only training was in the school of fig-tree pruning and Jacob was a liar, a cheat and a thief.

Solomon was too rich. Jesus was too poor. Abraham was too old. Peter was afraid of men's opinion and Lazarus was dead. Naomi was a widow. Paul was a persecutor of the church.

Jonah ran from God's will. Miriam was a gossip. Gideon and Thomas both doubted God's word and His voice. Jeremiah was depressed and suicidal. Elijah was burned out and ready to call it quits. John the Baptist was a loudmouth. Martha was a worry-wart, a workaholic and a basic type-A personality and Noah got drunk.

Thankfully for them and us, God doesn't require a job interview for salvation and He already knew what we were going to do and become before we allowed Him to save us from ourselves.

Everything belongs to Him, so He isn't concerned about our financial wealth or our educational accomplishments. God's not into body image, so He doesn't care what size your dress is a 2, 12, 22 or 32. Your pants can be a 28, 38 or 48 waist—as long as you're taking care of the temple in which He lives.

He knows who we are and what we are because He made us that way. We are fearfully and wonderfully made, and all of God's works are wonderful, (*Psalms 139:14.*)

Why don't we place the same level of value on our gifts, talents and abilities as God does? There are several reasons; first we compare ourselves to others. When we see other people's gifts, talents and abilities, we think ours are miniscule in comparison. We try to keep our gifts to ourselves so we won't look stupid or get our feelings hurt when we "don't quite measure up," (*Galatians 6:4.*)

In reality, our gifts are admired by many people, some we don't even know. God has purposed that they, our gifts, will make room for us in places where we never thought we'd be able to go, (*Proverbs 18:16.*)

We often wish we could do things we see other people do like sing or preach, but God doesn't call us to play the would'da, should'da, could'da game. God calls us to obey His commands and fulfill the destiny that He placed in us (*I Corinthians 7:7; Romans 12:6.*) And for a moment, consider this; would you be willing to go through what the other person went through in order to walk in the gift that's theirs? Would you be willing to miss the games or not hang out with your friends in order to go to piano or voice lesions, and work to perfect your gift? Would you be willing to over look being overlooked in order to fulfill the call to the ministry of helps?

Would you be willing to prophesy something to a friend that was not good news? Would you be willing to lay-hands on a street person and ask God to deliver them? Would you be willing to not have close friends because of your call to the ministry?

If you said "yes" to any of the aforementioned questions, then what are you doing to perfect your gifts? You see it's easy to say "yes I would" when it's not yours, but are we willing to be obedient to God when it comes to our own gifts, talents and abilities? Are we willing to give up television and the Internet in order to perfect our gifts? What are we willing to do to render unto God what He's given us?

Another reason we may not value our gifts to the level that we should is sometimes, we care more about what others think of us then what God thinks of us. As children of God, it's more important to please God rather than man, (*Acts 5:29.*) Pleasing God is a lot easier than pleasing man. There's only one God, when He tells you something there are no second or third opinions. His is the only voice you need to listen to for directions. But, when you listen to what people say, whose voice is more important? Your parents, your spouse, your children's, your bosses, your co-workers, your friends? And if it's friends, which one? To make one person happy, you've got to make another one unhappy. In order to keep one friend, you may have to loose another. When you try to please men, things can become very complicated.

People may say we're "different," "weird" or "don't quite fit in." We should rejoice in this, since the Lord said we would be a peculiar (chosen) people, (*I Peter 2:9* KJV—meaning, we have been chosen, purchased, bought with a price; therefore, we are not our own any more. We belong to the Lord.) All too often, instead of rejoicing in the truth of our redemption and our uniqueness in Christ we get upset when we don't fit in with a world that is dying daily.

Most of us want to fit in; it's comfortable and we want people to like us. We don't want to be different because being different—having different ideas, ideals, standards and moral codes—set us apart from other people and may cause us to be perceived as someone who is not acceptable by the standards of the world, (*John 15:19.*)

But Jesus, our example, lived in His own individuality. He never tried to be something He wasn't nor, did he apologize for what He was. He did not need other people to understand, agree or give approval of His life, the choices He made or the company He kept.

Jesus was clear; His only objective was to do the will of God, (*John 6:38.*) Keeping that key piece of information in the forefront of our minds will help us to remember to whom we owe our lives, our health and our strength.

God loves diversity. He wants His people to be different, not to fit into the world system. He doesn't even expect us to fit into a cookie cutter mold of each other, (*I Corinthians 12:7 – 11.*) He wants us to be and to become the part of His image He's placed in us individually, (*Philippians 3: 12 – 14,*) in order to take our rightful place in the Body of Christ.

On a baseball team you have nine defensive positions. All are equally important, but the pitchers gets the most attention because if he can throw the ball well enough that the batter can't hit the ball, then the other players don't have to worry about catching, fielding or throwing the ball. If the pitcher pitches well enough, the ball never enters the playing field.

What would a baseball team look like if everyone wanted to pitch so they could get the glory and the spotlight? Nine men gathered on the mound all trying to pitch the same ball. The real pitcher would not be able to do his job because his other eight team mates would be in the way. When the batter hit the ball, who would catch it? All the outfielders would be on the mound trying to do a job that's not their responsibility.

That's what we in the Body of Christ look like when we're all trying to do the same type of job rather than taking care of the job that coincides with the gifts, talents and abilities that we've been given to steward.

Another reason we don't operate in our gifts, talents and abilities maybe that we don't really trust that God has our best interest at heart.

What He's asked us to do is so far fetched, that we can't fully wrap our brains around it. God never asked us to wrap our brains around what He's told us to do. He's told us to wrap our actions around what He's told us to do, (*Luke 11:28; Jeremiah 7:23; Jeremiah 10:23.*)

Abraham was called away from everything he knew and everything that would have rightfully been his in the future, by a God he didn't know, couldn't see, feel or touch, but yet he trusted this unknown God enough to leave it all for the unknown.

Abraham walked away from his past—His accessorial history and their traditions. He left behind "how we've always done it" and walked into, "I don't know what to do, or how to do it." He awaited instructions from God, made mistakes and had to leave friends and family behind, but he followed God.

One of my favorite hobbies is baking and decorating cakes. Both my Grandmothers baked and taught me the little tricks bakers use to make cakes special. I've never thought of baking as an art or anything that required creativity. I don't even consider myself a good baker, it's something I enjoy and I can share the fruits of my labor with friends and family.

A few years ago, I found myself in a situation of a "temporary interruption of cash flow." That's a cute way of saying I was in need of some additional funds. I decided that I was going to take a second job for a while and began inquiring at businesses near my home about part-time work.

I've been in the administrative support field for years and have great clerical stills. I have a home office already set up with the latest technology and gadgets. With the advances in remote access and my years of experience, I just knew finding work I could do from home wouldn't be a problem, but I was wrong. No agency work was forthcoming, but somehow God kept making a way. Not from one month to another, but from one day to another.

Some friends and I had decided to attend a

weekend workshop session hosted by Bishop T.D. Jakes. One workshop discussed building financial wealth. The woman who was facilitating the presentation said, "I know that everyone in here can do something to make an extra one hundred dollars a month."

As I set there, I began to pray for God to open the door for my clerical work. My friend LaVerne was with me and she too has many years experience in the administrative field and we began to talk about how we could make this work. How could we market our skills sets and years of experience? Just as LaVerne and I finished our brainstorming session, the Lord spoke to my heart and said "You can bake cakes."

I thought *What?, Bake cakes? Me? Who would I sell them to? Why would anyone want to buy a cake from me?* Then, God laid out the plan. Thankfully I had enough good sense to write down the plan as God revealed it.

How shocked was I when I realized people were willing to pay me to make them cakes. I've even taken classes to find out what I would need to do business on a larger scale. I believed that if it is God's will, my baking will become the primary vehicle for my income.

What I needed to meet me at my point of need was right inside of me.

Finally, some of us have not placed our gifts in God's hands because we're afraid of what He may do with them. We are also fearful of what He might ask us do with them so that he maybe glorified.

Some of us have not placed our talents in God's hands because we still think we can do something with them ourselves. But the vast majority of us have not placed our gifts, talent and abilities in God's hand because we don't know what God placed in our hands.

In third chapter of Philippians, Paul is discussing his past life as a "Jew's Jew" and relating it to where he was spiritually at the time of the writing. He makes a statement in verse 12 that he is moving toward becoming "that for which Christ took hold of me." What does that mean? It means that in the eternity before this time period, when God created you and me, He placed some things in us that Jesus wants to use in His body. That's why Christ took hold of us, so that the gifts, talents and abilities that God placed in us can be used for the betterment of the Body of Christ. So the question becomes what should we be moving toward becoming?

Many of us for one reason or another never got an opportunity to explore all our hopes and dreams. While that is disheartening and often quite depressing, it doesn't mean that we don't have anything to offer. In the 12th chapter of I Corinthians, Paul states that the Holy Spirit gives everyone at least one gift. What is your gift? It may be singing or teaching, it may be helping others or administration. No matter what it is, it is the reason Christ "took hold of you."

Don't compare yourself to others. Many times we see people operate in gifts that put them out front, the gift of tongues, etc. - SO WHAT?! Read *I Corinthians 12* at the end when Paul is ranking the gifts we should aspire to have you'll see the gift of tongues is at the very bottom of the totem pole.

Your gifts, talents and abilities are why Christ took hold of YOU, not why He took hold of me or anyone else. He needs your gifts and my gifts in order for His Body to function at its optimum performance level. This is why the Body of Christ is so crippled today; everyone wants someone else's anointing rather than gaining Godly knowledge, wisdom and understanding about their own.

What if you don't know what your gift, talent or ability is? In James the first chapter, James states that if someone lacks wisdom, let him or her ask God for wisdom and He will give it freely. Ask God for wisdom. Ask God, not your friends or your family members because they didn't give you your gifts, talents or abilities. Go to the source of the gift, go to the creator of the talent, and go to the sustainer of the ability. Go to God. If you operate in a talent, ability or gift but you know in your Spirit person there's something more, go to God and ask for wisdom. God will give you clarity.

Don't have much to offer? Just remember, "Little becomes much, when you place it in the Master's hands." His hands are always open, ready to receive what we want to give Him.

PRAYER:

Lord, please help me to see my gifts, talents and abilities as you see them. Help me Lord to lean on you, the author, perfecter and finisher of my faith, and not on my own understanding or what other people say about me. Help me Father, to understand the great power you placed in me at the time I accepted you, the power that allows me to be self-sufficient in Christ's sufficiency. Lord, renew my mind so that I understand that there is nothing too difficult for you to perform through me if I yield all my members to you. You are my strength and my shield. Thank you Lord, Amen.

Little Becomes Much - Part II

What Do You Have to Lose?

II King 4:1-7

In the story of the widow and the oil, the widow had her back against the wall. Her husband was dead. She was in hock up to her nose. The man to whom she is indebted was coming to enslaving her sons. In her opinion, she had nothing of value that could get her out of the predicament she was facing.

Many of us can relate to the situation the widow found herself. Nothing was going right. Everything seemed to be closing in on her at the same time. She had run out of options and nothing could bail her out so...she turned to God.

The text doesn't say she prayed. It says she went to the prophet. In other words, she went to the man of God. She left where she was and moved by faith to find, Elisha, the man of God.

What if he hadn't been in town? What if he had been too busy to come and see about her needs? What if he had been preoccupied with someone or something more important?

Thank God we have Jesus!!! We never have to worry about Him not being around. He is Jehovah Shammah; the Lord *is* there. When ever we need for Jesus to speak to us, all we have to do is pick up the Bible. In the first chapter of Hebrews, Paul states that God used to talk to His people through the prophets. But now, He speaks to us through His Son; who John declared is the Word of God, who became flesh and came to dwell among mankind, (*John 1:1 – 2, 14.*)

We have access to the throne room of God by the blood of Jesus Christ, (*Romans 5:1 – 2.*) We have a standing invitation to come to God because we are joint heirs with Christ, (*Romans 8:17.*) God has an open door policy with us, His sons and daughters, because of our relationship with His only begotten son Jesus, (*Hebrews 4:15 – 16.*)

Since Elisha and all the prophets of the Old Testament are a picturing of Jesus, we should treat Jesus the same way this woman treated the prophet. First, she went to him for insight and for help. She didn't go to her pew partner or her prayer partner; she went to the man of God. Secondly, she obeyed what he told her to do.

We should go to Jesus first. Not our Pastor's, not our friends. Jesus, the word of God, should be the very first place we turn. Then, once we get the solution we should obey. No questions or doubts, just obey. The Word of God says that we should be anxious for nothing, but through prayer with praise and thanksgiving let our request be known to God, (*Philippians 4:6 – 7.*)

It doesn't matter if you've been down this road before, if Jesus is giving you a new path, asking you to do something you haven't done before to resolve your problem, do it. In *Isaiah 46:10*, it says God makes known the end from the beginning. His purpose will stand and He will do as he pleases. In other words, He knows just what's going on and is willing to tell you, but you've got to be willing to listen and obey if you want God's will to stand in your life.

The widow didn't have a long conversation with Elisha. She didn't argue with him and tell him how his plan wasn't going to work. She didn't hesitate or procrastinate. She simply obeyed. I mean, what did she have to lose?

The man she was indebted to was going to come and take her sons if she didn't pay him, so what was the worse thing that could happen if she followed what Elisha told her? What Elisha told her may not have worked, but she would have been no worse off at the end then she was when she began the process.

What Elisha told her to do was *not* a sure thing. It sounded crazy and it didn't make any sense. But the she did it anyway. The widow did two things that many of us won't do. First, she took a risk. She had not guarantees and no precedence to rely on. All she had was an impossible possibility. Second, she took God at His word. She didn't ask for a sign. She didn't stop to pray. She didn't ask for a second opinion. She didn't call anyone and tell them what she was going to do, she just obeyed.

When the widow went to Elisha, he asked her two questions. 1. What do you want me to do for you? 2. What do you have in your house? Strange questions? Not really. What the prophet wanted to know was; are you willing to do what I tell you to do in order to help yourself? And, what do you have, and are willing to give, to start the process of moving from little too much?

Many of us have a lot of gifts, talents and abilities that we could use in order to bless our own houses, but we won't use them because we're afraid of what others may think or say. Many of us have been given instructions by the Lord that would move us to our wealthy place, but because we've never seen or heard of anything like what God is telling us to do or we're concerned that we'll fail, we sit on it, paralyzed because we can't use one of our five human senses to make sense of what God is revealing to us.

Right now, God is asking you those same questions. "_____ (insert your name)_____, are you willing to do what I've told you to do in order to help yourself? And, _____ (insert your name) _____, what do you have, and are willing to give, to start the process of moving from little too much?"

The widow replied, "I have nothing, but a little oil." Then, Elisha told her what to do and she obeyed him.

This woman was putting her future in her own hands at the instruction of the man of God. She had nowhere else to turn, nothing else she could do. She was as desperate for an answer as some of us say we are. If she gave him everything she had left, her "little" oil, and he blew it, what would she do? The same thing she would do if she kept it without acknowledging it was there. She would lose everything she had including her future, because remember her sons, her future, were going to be enslaved to pay off her debt.

What do you have to lose? If God tells you to give up that "little thing" like your pride, what do you have to lose? If he tells you to give up that "little thing" like your voice, your ability to play an instrument or your ability to write, what do you have to lose? If he tells you to give up that boyfriend or that girlfriend, what do you have to lose?

Some of us are looking at our circumstances. We need money, but when we look at our checkbooks and savings accounts we don't see money, so we say the same thing the widow said: "I have debts, doubts, difficulties and am in need of deliverance. Jesus, help me I have nothing in my house but..." Jesus says, "That will do if you put it all in my hands and obey my words," (*Luke 11:28.*)

To put something in someone else's hands means you no longer have ownership of it. To put something in someone else's hands means you no longer have mastery of it. It now belongs, lock, stock and barrel, to the person whose hands you put it in. What's that "little thing" you have in your house? Maybe it's none of those things named above, maybe it's "just" the gift of gab. Maybe it's "just" the gift to make a child smile or maybe it's "just" the gift to listen until someone else feels better. Whatever it is, no matter how small, are you willing to put it in Jesus' hands so He can add the increase?

Remember, no matter how big you think your talent, gift or ability is if it's not in God's hands it's small, limited and traceable to you. Traceable to you? Yes, everyone can trace it right back to you and God gets no glory.

What "little thing" do you have in your house? Whatever it is, turn it over to God. What do you have to lose?

PRAYER

God, the Father of heaven and earth, show me what I have in my life that I can give to you to help your people. Lord, help me to see beyond the obvious and look past what I see with my natural eye. Help me Savior, to know and understand through Godly wisdom that I have been ordained by You for service and that I have gifts, talents and abilities that can be utilized by you, to help further your kingdom here on earth. And then Lord, after you have shown me what it is that I have that you want to use, give me the courage to use it for you. Give me your strength and endurance and I will fulfill your will for my life. I believe that you will and thank you for your faithfulness to your word for me in my life. Amen.

Little Becomes Much – Part III
Your Oil Is in Your House
II King 4:1-7

When I was growing up I used to hear older saints talk about people who thought they could just copy someone else in the church and they would be empowered by the Holy Spirit like the person they were imitating. Sometimes people went as far as dressing like the person they were imitating to try to get the Holy Spirit to move them the way He moved someone else.

You still have this going on in church today. You can go to some churches and see ministers and wanna-be ministers acting "like," trying to preach "like" and even trying to look "like" someone you see when you turn on your television. How could this happen in the Body of Christ? Generally, it's because we're looking outside our houses for what we think we need.

When the widow went to Elisha, he asked her what do you have in your house. The answer was she had some oil. She didn't talk about what she could get from her friends or family members and Elisha didn't ask her what was at her disposal from someone else. Why? Because Elisha knew that everything she needed she already in her house.

Anytime you see oil mentioned in the Bible it is a picturing of the anointing of the Holy Spirit. So, the widow could have said, "I have nothing in my house, but a little anointing." A little anointing of the Holy Spirit goes a long way.

Remember, that the Holy Spirit gave each of us gifts for use in the Body of Christ. Our ability to use the gifts, talents or abilities come from the anointing sealed in us by the Holy Spirit when we accept Christ. We all have an anointing to do something because everyone has at least one gift, (*I Corinthians 12:11.*)

But we also know that no man is an island. No man stands alone. In our own bodies would an eye pull out and say "I'm doing this all by myself, I don't need any of you?" Of course not. So it is in the Body of Christ, (*I Corinthians 12:24b – 27.*) We each have at least one function within the Body of Christ, but if we're not using our anointing or operating in our proper place, then the Body of Christ is crippled and operating in a mode of affliction.

What is your gift? What are your talents? Not everyone one can be a preacher or a teacher, (*I Timothy 3:1-13.*) Not everyone can be a leader in the church, but everyone has a gift, and without everyone operating in their gifts, the leadership of the church and its ministries are hampered. You end up with a church that is out of balance. You have too few people trying to do too much, all because you have too many people not trying to do anything.

What has God anointed your hands to do for your local church congregation? What has He anointed you to do for the Christian community at large? Whatever it is stop letting yourself; your past history, your failures, your triumphs, your current circumstances and situations, delay God's plan to move you into the place He has already ordained you will operate.

It may not be comfortable, but it's doable through Christ who has given you the strength to do what He has anointed you to do.

The widow only went to her neighbors because she was told too. The text does not say that she told them what she was doing or why she needed the jars. Sometimes we need to keep some things that God has called us to do to ourselves until He releases us to tell other people.

The only people around her during the entire process were her sons. In verse four, Elisha tells the widow, "Then go inside and shut the door behind you and your sons." They, like she, had a vested interested in making sure the instructions from the man of God were carried out. There are times when God shuts us away from everyone and everything else because what He wants to do for us is so miraculous, so great, so awesome He can't let anyone who isn't directly affected by what's going on be involved. When this happens, don't fret— rejoice. God is going to do a great thing!!!

This women who had nothing but "a little oil" walked in faith from the moment she went to the Prophet until she filled the last jar without questioning the rational of what she had been assigned. Imagine what would have happened if she had over analyzed or tried to put human reason to what the Elisha had told her. I believe she would have ended up like many of us; frustrated, angry about her half finished work and in a worse position then when she started the initial process.

The widow did not deviate from what the man of God told her to do. She followed his instructions until the task that she had been assigned was complete. She didn't start anything new. She didn't add to her "to do list." She allowed her oil (her anointing) to flow in one direction until God changed the direction.

How often do we start down the road the Lord has designated for us only to be distracted by other people asking us to do things that aren't in-line with what God has asked or told us to do? In fact, what the people are asking us to do is going to take us off target of what God asked us to do.

There is one simple word we've got to learn to use when we're moving to fulfill our destiny in Christ. The word is "NO."

"Can you serve as team Mom?" NO. "Can you sit on the hospitality ministry at church?" NO. "Can you work on the PTA?" NO. "Can you direct the choir until we find someone to do it full-time?" NO.

If what other people are asking you to do isn't going to enhance, encourage or help engage you in what the Lord has asked you to do, the answer has to be "no." Don't get distracted. Stay focused on the task that God has given you.

The widow didn't go back to Elisha for further instructions until the first task had been completed. All the jars she had had been filled and the oil had stopped flowing. She had sown her seed of faith and now it was time for her to reap the harvest.

"Go, sell the oil and pay your debts. You and yours sons can live on what is left." Just like that, God has supplied all her needs and in abundance. God didn't just pay off her debt, but because of her obedience she had an overflow and what she needed for her miracle was in her own house all along.

Some of you will say that the widow had to go outside her house and get the jars, so what she needed for her miracle wasn't in her house, you're wrong!!! What she needed for her miracle was in her house. She needed the oil. She didn't sell the jars, she sold the oil. The jars were just used to contain what was going to bless her and her sons. The jars were not the blessing.

What do you have in your house that you can give to God to use for your benefit? Whatever it is, don't belittle it. Cherish it and by faith allow God to nurture it and watch it bless you in a supernatural way.

Have you followed the instructions God has given you without question? If not, it's not too late. Start now. Begin to get rid of distractions and cut out things that aren't going to help you reach your pre-ordained destiny in Christ.

PRAYER

Father, whatever oil you have given me for my house, I now pledge to use it for your kingdom building purposes. I will no longer sit back and watch and wonder what I could do, or lament over what I haven't done, but I will press forward to the higher mark in Christ Jesus.

I will seek your face Lord, your face I will seek for the purpose of bringing me closer to You so that in all things in my life you will be glorified, I may be edified and the enemy will be nullified. I do not operate in the spirit of fear disguised by reasons, logic or excuses, but I walk in the knowledge of the power that has dwelled in me for the purpose of doing your bidding.

Thank you for choosing me. Amen.

Oh, What a Friend!

John 15:14 - "You are my friends if you do what I command."

Friends have things in common. A shared interest like, shopping, eating out, sports, books, hobbies; something that cause them to be drawn together—hence they get to know each other and begin to share with each other. Out of that sharing a friendship emerges.

Over time, a simple friendship turns to a closer relationship until there forms a mutual level of knowledge about each others character traits, likes, dislikes. You get to know each others concerns, strengths and weaknesses. And often, you see your friend's gifts, talents and abilities better than they do, which enables you to encourage them when they think less of themselves then they should.

One of my best friend's name is LaVerne. When my family and I moved to Maryland she attended our church and went to Bible study with me and sang on the choir, but our relationship was nurtured outside of church because her daughter and my son were in class together; which meant we attended PTA meetings and other school functions.

Our children became fast friends and wanted to spend a lot of time together, which meant LaVerne and I spent a lot of time together. At church, at school and in outside activities it seemed that almost everything we did involved the other.

Our friendship began because of our children, but over the 11 years that we've known each other our children's friendship has grown further apart, but LaVerne's and my friendship keeps getting closer and closer.

Over those 11 years we've seen good and bad times. Agreed to disagree; discovered our passions and gifts; used our passions and gifts to help each other and grown closer to the Lord.

This is how it should be with our relation with Christ. No matter where or how we were introduced to Him, we ought to spend enough time with Him to cause our relationship to grow stronger no matter how long it's been or how much we've been through.

In a real friendship there is correction. Friends don't let friends do things that are going to hurt them or other people without working to correct their actions. Real friends tell the truth. Whether it's something small like how someone looks in a dress or whether they've gained weight or lost too much. Or, if it's something big like their emotions are out of sorts or the way they are treating their children or spouse is not Godly. Real friends, get in their friends business.

Friends don't tell "complimentary lies." What is a

complimentary lie? Let me give you an example: Your friend sings a solo at church and they really don't sing well at all. They were out of tune, off pitch and all together wreck the song. When it's over everyone is standing around telling your friend, "That was beautiful." "Oh, I didn't know you could sing so well." "Ahhh, you really have a voice."

Often times we do this because we don't want to tell the person how bad they sounded or that we didn't enjoy their singing, but what we don't realize is that we're doing more harm than good.

A friend wants their friends to operate in their God-given gifts. If singing is not their God-given gift they should continue to look for what God has for them and not settle for what they want for themselves. By giving "complimentary lies" we are encouraging our friend to do something that may not be in God's plan for them. We may be helping them go down a path not intended for them and leading them away from where God wants them.

I Corinthians 7:7b say: "But each man has his own gift from God one has this gift, another has that." Why would you want your friend to operate in a gift that is not theirs? Wouldn't you want your friend to tell you the truth? Real friends don't give "complimentary lies" they give gentle truths.

Jesus came to give me the ability to have a friendship with God. Jesus came and gave me holiness so I can have a friendship with a holy God. Jesus became my righteousness so I can have it in common with the only righteous God. Jesus came to give me the mind of God, so I can understand the secrets of His Word and live in truth. Jesus came to give me eternal life, so that I can live forever with my friend, God.

Jesus came to elevate me so I can be a friend of God, but He did not come to lessen God so He can be my friend.

Jesus did not come and make God my Genie in the bottle, my friend only to grant my wishes. Jesus did not come to compromise God so that you and I can live any way we want and still call ourselves Christians. Jesus did not come to lower God's standards to the world standards. NO!!! Jesus came to elevate us to God's will for our lives.

It is because of Jesus that we have a friendship with God, but understand God is always going to be greater.

His standard is always right. Ours aren't.

His word is always true and His promises always kept. Ours aren't.

God has never and won't ever make a mistake. We make mistakes every day.

Gods' will has always and will always prevail. Ours won't.

Gods' way has always been and will always be perfect. Ours is not.

Gods' decisions are based on the whole picture of live and lives. Ours decisions are generally structured around ourselves and our limited knowledge of the whole picture.

Jesus came to make me friends with God, but not equivalent to God. Wanting to be equivalent to God was Satan's problem. In *Isaiah 14:14*, Lucifer makes this statement, "I will ascend about the tops of the clouds; I will make myself like the Most High." Lucifer learned first hand that "pride goes before destruction, a haughty spirit before a fall," (*Proverbs 16:18.*)

In *Ezekiel 28:2*, God address the issue of anyone being God other than Himself. "Son of man, say to the ruler of Tyre, 'This is what the Sovereign Lord says: "In the pride of your heart you say, 'I am a god: I sit on the throne of a god in the heart of the seas.' But you are a man and not a god, though you think you are as wise as a god.'"

No one is God, but God. No matter how much we prayer, how many times per week we fast, how many ministries we sit over in church or how much money we give to the poor, we are not gods.

We are sinners, saved by grace and given new mercies every day by the unmerited favor of God through Christ. If we were gods we wouldn't have needed Jesus to come and die for our sins and to save us from an eternal separation from God's love, peace and power.

Our role model of living a life of friendship with God is Jesus. Jesus spent quality time with God. He counseled with God about decisions. He walked humbly before the Lord. Jesus only spoke what He was taught by the Father. And, He cared for others more then Himself

Luke 22:39 – 41 states "Jesus went out as usual to the Mount of Olives, and his disciples followed him. On reaching the place, he said to them, "Pray that you will not fall into temptation." He withdrew about a stone's throw beyond them, knelt down and prayed." Jesus loved his disciples, but He relished spending time with the Father by Himself.

In Luke 6:12 – 13, scripture says – "One of those days Jesus went out to a mountainside to pray, and spent the night praying to God. When morning came, he called his disciples to him and chose twelve of them, whom he also designated apostles." In other words, Jesus counseled with God before He made decisions.

In *John 5:30* Jesus is speaking and says, "By myself I can do nothing: I judge only as I hear, and my judgment is just, for I seek not to please myself but him who sent me." Jesus had humbled Himself to God to the point that His will no longer mattered. But in return, He was given the right to judge everything justly because He was judging it through the eyes of God and not His own selfish motives.

In *John 22:42* Jesus was in the Garden of Gethsemane, and he told the Father, "if you are willing, take this cup from me; yet not my will, but yours be done." Even though Jesus was in great anguish and an angel had to come and strengthen him, Jesus cared more about us then He did his own life and He went to the cross and died for us.

Jesus' death was not about his friendship with the Father, it was about our friendship with the Father. Jesus knew unless He died and atoned for the sins of the world, we would never have the opportunity to be reconciled with God and never have the ability to form a friendship with our Creator.

Jesus did the hard work regarding our relationship with God. He bought our salvation by

His sacrifice. It is our responsibility to nurture our relationship with God and cultivate our friendship with Him by following Jesus' example of spending time with God, placing God in the midst of all our decisions, walking humbly before Him, only doing what God tells us to do and caring more about others then we do ourselves.

Isn't it a blessing to be able to sing the old spiritual that says – "What a friend we have in Jesus? All our sins and grieves to bear. What a privilege to carry, everything to God in pray."

PRAYER

Father God, in the name of Jesus I thank you for being my friend. I know that you're my friend because of the finished work of Christ Jesus. I know that Jesus came to give me all the qualities necessary to allow me to come into friendship with you, but you and I are not peers.

You are my friend because of your great love for me, not because of anything I've ever done. You care about our friendship because you created me to be like you. You're my friend because life can be hard and cruel and I need someone to whom I can turn and put my trust. Thank you Lord for your friendship, your love, your compassion your mercy and your grace.

In Jesus name I pray, amen.

What Do You Do When "Christians" Hurt You?

Matthew 19:18 – 19 "Jesus replied, "Do not murder, do not commit adultery, do not steal, do not give false testimony, honor your father and mother, and 'love your neighbor as yourself.'"

When I was growing up, I believed that everyone who went to church was saved. I believed that every preacher and teacher was anointed and ordained by God to carry out His mission.

But that was many years and many hurts ago. I've found that sometimes the very people you should be able to turn to in times of trouble, difficulties and pain are the very ones who cause you trouble, bring about difficulties and inflict the pain.

So what do you do when saints hurt you? Where do you turn to ease the ache in your heart? You turn to and lean on the only wise God.

Easier said than done, right? Here are a few passages of scripture that can help you get through until your change comes.

1. Know that the person hurt you and NOT GOD.

Satan wants nothing more than to move you out of a right relationship with God, under the guise of what a saint (or ain't) did, but don't let him have the victory. In *John 1 0: 1 0* (KJV) Jesus declares that he came "to give you life, and that more abundantly." The life He's talking about isn't just physical life but more importantly, a spiritual life. Paul explains it further *Galatians 2:20,* "I have been crucified with Christ and I no longer live, but Christ lives in me. The life I live in the body, I live by faith in the Son of God, who loved me and gave himself for me."

This is the kind of life that gets you through the day when you would rather have died, the kind of life that makes you get up and move, when you would rather wallow in self-pity.

This kind of life only comes from the power of the Holy Spirit that lives in each born again believer. *Acts 1:8A* states, "But you will receive power when the Holy Spirit comes on you..."

2. Don't get even, get obedient

Romans 12:19 says, "Do not take revenge, my friend, but leave room for God's wrath, for it is written: "It is mine to avenge, I will repay,"says the Lord.'" If you want God to work on your behalf, you have to do it His way.

You can't go behind people back and talk about them; you can't try to get anyone to dislike the person that has mistreated you. No gossiping or backbiting. And you should be very careful about with whom you discuss the situations, because additional people can make a bad situation even worse.

The principle of sowing and reaping will take over. "Do not be deceived, God is not mocked, whatever a man (or woman) sows that shall he (she) also reap," (Galatians 6:7,) and "He who sows wickedness reaps trouble," (*Proverbs 22:8A.*)

Remember, God cannot lie; if He said it, it will happen. It may look like the offender is getting away with hurting you. It may seem that God is not avenging His elect, but hold on and don't give up.

God must do what He said He will do, but WE must be obedient to His word and not try to hurt the person who hurt us, or let everybody know what they did.

God's word will not return to Him void, but it will accomplish exactly what He sent it to do. Do it God's way and watch Him move.

3. Don't Lose Focus

No one was more tired of hearing about turning the other cheek than me. I used to say to me, *How many cheeks does God think I have?* But what that scripture really means is summed up in *Romans 12:21* "Do not be overcome by evil, but overcome evil with good."

Don't let hate and anger slip into your heart and

cause you to sin because of what happened. Don't worry about what happened, don't fret yourself over it. Don't dwell on it and cause yourself to start acting out of your emotions. This is what Satan wants. He knows if he can get your mind on the person, situation or circumstance, you will sin.

Why will you sin? Because you can only think about one thing at a time. If your mind is on the action of the other person or what their action caused to occur in your life, then you mind can't be on Christ.

Don't lose focus on the solution. Christ is the solution. The word of God is your solution.

Jesus gave us peace. Peace is a part of the fruit of the Spirit. You don't have to ask for it, because you already have it. You have to learn to walk in it. Christ is the center of our joy and He has given us joy to accompany our peace. He is our focus. He is our example.

Think of Jesus and the Pharisees, the Sadducees and the Scribes. You didn't see Jesus hanging out with them. He took care of the necessary business He had with them and left them alone. But, when they came to Him for help and guidance, He didn't turn them away, (*John 3.*)

In closing, I know these situations can be trying, but no matter what happens or has happened, we are to love one another, as we love ourselves. Jesus knew Judas was going to betray Him, (*John 13:27,*) but that didn't stop Him from treating Judas the same as all the other disciples when he was having the Passover Supper with them and washing their feet.

In the same way, we must treat all those who are in the Body of Christ with love, compassion and understanding, doing for them what Christ did for us. He overlooked our offenses and met our needs.

PRAYER

Lord, I am hurt and wounded by the act of someone else in the Body of Christ. Heal the heartache and take away the pain. Let me see them as you see them. Lord search my heart; where there is bitterness replace it with compassion. Where there is resentment, replace it with Godly understanding. Where there is dislike or discontentment, replace it with your love, the love that covers a multitude of sins. Remind me Lord, that you are my help. Your name is my strong tower and because I am made righteous through you, I can run into your name and be saved. I rejoice in You Lord and what you are doing in me, even right now. Amen.

Who's Singing to the Prisoners?

Acts 15:16 - 34

Acts 15:25 states, "About midnight Paul and Silas were praying and singing hymns to God, and the other prisoners were listening to them." The other prisoners weren't singing praises and praying to God. Either because they didn't have the same belief system as Paul and Silas or they weren't as mature in Christ as these two great men of the gospel, and therefore didn't sing because they didn't feel like they had a reason to sing.

Here are Paul and Silas; they had been attacked by a crowd, the authorities ordered they be stripped and severely flagged and then thrown into prison with their feet in stocks. From all outward appearance it didn't appear that Paul and Silas had much to sing about either, but Paul and Silas' joy didn't come from outward circumstances. Their joy came from their love of Jesus and out of that love; they had a sincere desire to show other people the goodness of the Lord through their lives.

Paul and Silas had a lot to be upset about, they

were being obedient to the word and the will of God and showing the love of the Lord to others. They weren't hurting anyone, they were helping. They weren't causing trouble, they were showing compassion. They weren't trying to change the government systems, just the eternal home of other people, but yet they were not accepted by the masses.

In *John 15:19*, Jesus says – "If you belonged to the world, it would love you as its own. As it is, you do not belong to the world, but I have chosen you out of the world. That is why the world hates you." Paul and Silas knew that the world would not understand why they were compelled to do the will of the Lord, but that didn't stop them.

In or out of jail, Paul and Silas let a dying world know that Jesus cared for them. They didn't not pick and chose who they thought was worthy of being told about the goodness of God. Paul and Silas didn't play gods by saying who they would or would not preach the gospel to.

No, they believed *John 3:16*, "For God so loved the world that He gave His only begotten son, and WHO SOEVER believes in Him will not perish, but have everlasting life." They also understood it was their responsibility to fulfill the great commission, "Therefore go and make disciples of all nations, baptizing them in the name of the Father and of the Son and of the Holy Spirit, and teaching them to obey everything I have commanded you," (*Matthew 28:19 – 20A*.) It was not their place to allow their personal biases to stop them from singing to all the prisoners.

We often send e-mails about Christ to each other in order to build each other up. We send gospel words of encouragement to brothers and sisters in the Lord, but what do we send to those people that we know do not know the freedom of knowing Christ? What do we give to those who are not in the body of Christ, who need to know that through Christ all our binds can be broken? How many of us sing to the prisoners that we know?

We all know that prisons aren't just places were criminals go when they get caught doing something that's against the law. Anyone who is not in Christ is a prisoner of the law of sin and death. We have family members, friends and co-workers who are prisoners. We know people who suffer from anxiety, depression and low self-esteem, but for some reason we often find it hard to reach out to them with the love of Christ to say, "I know a man who will love you back to wholeness. Can I tell you what he's done for me?"

Do you live you're life in a state of praise and glory to God or do you find yourself grumbling, murmuring and complaining like the people who don't know Christ? If we react the same way they do to bad news or hurtful situations, how will they ever know that Christ can make a difference in their life?

No, you don't have to be fake, but you have an everlasting hope in Christ Jesus, do you act like it? You are guaranteed a place in heaven when this phase of life is complete, do you act like you're looking forward to it or do you act just as lost and dejected as a sinner?

Paul and Silas were in the same predicament as the other prisoners, maybe even worse, but they didn't have the same mind set. They had a mind set of praise to God in the midst of the trial. They had a mind set of giving God glory in middle of a dark situation. They had a mind set of letting other people know that they had hope through Christ, even in what appeared to be a hopeless situation. Paul and Silas not only encourage themselves, but everyone who could hear them. Who have you encouraged lately?

Paul and Silas could have whispered, but they chose to sing out so that the OTHER prisoners could hear them. What was going to affect the prisoners, who may have been in sin, was going to affect Paul and Silas too, even though they were in Christ. Don't think so? Look at the earthquake. It shook the whole prison, not just Paul and Silas' cell.

Everyone's binds were loosed, not just Paul and Silas. Why is this important? Everyone who was within an ear shot of the songs of praise was affected. We need to come to a place of understanding that we don't walk this walk by ourselves, nor do we do walk it just for ourselves. There are others involved in what we do, even if they're just watching or listening to how we live our lives.

Now before you go off sending every e-mail you've ever gotten to every unsaved or "undersaved" friend or family member you know and have, remember every e-mail we get is not worth sending. Some e-mails we receive are chain letters, but we send them anyway. Some e-mail we receive have Jesus' name tattooed to them, but not scriptural, Biblically based nor Christ centered, but we send them anyway. And some e-mail we get is down right worldly, but we send them anyway.

We carry the title of "Ambassadors of Christ." Is that e-mail you're about to send something that Jesus would have anything to do with? Is it truly going to glorify and lift His name? Is it clear what message is being conveyed? If not, don't send it.

Remember *Colossians 3:23*, "Whatever you do, work at it with all your heart, as working for the Lord, not for men, since you know that you will receive an inheritance from the Lord as a reward. It is the Lord Christ you are serving." When you are at work, you should be working, not sending personal emails, not even ones about Christ.

When you're at work you should be working, not holding Bible study on the telephone. When you're at work you should be working, not surfing the web for non-job related things.

What kind of testimony is that to a sinner? You can use the time on your job to do things that aren't job related just because it's about Jesus? No. We want to uphold the rightness of God in all we do and every place we go; that way we can make sure that when we're talking to the unsaved or the "undersaved" about how Christ wants us to live our lives, they won't think of us as a Pharisee or a hypocrite.

Should we play Ms. and Mr. Polly and Peter Perfect? No, but we should hold up the standards that Christ as set for us everywhere we go, so when we begin to sing to the prisoners they're not hearing sour notes.

PRAYER:

Father, give me the boldness to proclaim you goodness to the lost of this world. Help me to live my life in such a way that others may see how good, kind, merciful and loving you are—not only to and for me, but to everyone who believes that Jesus is your only Son.

Father I realize that I as begin to talk to others about you, they are going to begin to look at how I'm living my life, help me not to give you a bad name because of my behavior. I know I won't be perfect until I met you in my eternal life, but help me to walk closer to you and more obediently so that my life gives you glory, even in difficult times and situations. Thank you Lord for your goodness and your grace, in Jesus name I pray, amen.

Whose Report – Part I
Satan's Report

Ephesians 3:17 – 19 "…and I pray that you, being rooted and established in love may have power together with all the saints, to grasp how wide and long and high and deep is the love of Christ, and to know this love that surpasses knowledge that you maybe filled to the measure of all the fullness of God."

I was on my way into the office the other morning with lots of stuff on my mind, and the Lord asked me a simple question, "Whose report do you believe?"

"Well, that's pretty easy" I said, "I believe the report of the Lord."

"Well, that's too easy," the Lord replied, "Did you know there are four reports you have to deal with when you need to make a decision or consider what to do?" And with that the Lord gave me a revelation lesson.

The scripture base is *Eph. 4:17*, "So I tell you this and insist on it in the Lord, that you must no longer live as the Gentiles do, in the futility of their thinking."

Conviction or Condemnation

There are two obvious reports, God's report which is always all truth and, Satan's report which is always a lie, even when he tells you something that sounds true and looks true you can rest assure it's a lie because he's doing it to condemn you and bring you to a place of guilt and shame.

Let me explain it like this. We fall short and sin against God; let's say we gossip about someone, or listen to someone else as they gossip. Satan comes along and says, "You know what you did was wrong, you had no right saying that about him/her, nor did you have any right listening while the other person talked about him/her. You should have stopped them, you shouldn't have allowed them to go on, you're a sinner, you're not the Christian you thought you were, you're not growing like you should, etc."

You may say that Satan is right, he's telling the truth. I shouldn't have done this or that. BUT, God judges the motive of everything and to God the truth of the matter is always the motive, (*Psalms 16:2*,) because the motive is from the heart and God judges the heart. What is Satan's motive for telling you about what you've done? His motive, out of his heart, is to condemn you and render you ineffective as a Christian by using guilt and shame to halt your progress and cause you to become so absorbed in what you did you can't get onto what God wants you to do.

What Satan doesn't tell you is Jesus died once, for all—all sin and for all time. Every sin that has ever been committed or ever will be committed has already been atoned for by the blood of Jesus. He died to take away the sins of the world, that's every sin. He did it once, for all time. But in order to walk in the freedom of Jesus' atoning sacrifice, you have to accept Jesus as Savior.

Where does the lie come in? *Romans 8: 1* says, "Therefore, there is no condemnation for those who are in Christ Jesus." A lie is anything that stands against the word of God. Anything that condemns you is a lie, because if you are in Christ, there is no condemnation. So, in all the "truth" that Satan was giving you, he lied because his purpose was to condemn you, and you can't be condemned if you are in Christ because your eternal life has been sealed by the Holy Spirit. God does not condemn us when we sin. He allows the Holy Spirit to convict us, so that we can turn away from the sin and repent.

Don't get condemnation mixed up with conviction. They are two very different things. The biggest difference is life and death. In the world, when a person stands trial and is found guilty of a crime, he or she is convicted. There is a penalty that has to be paid. It may be money, time in prison or public service, but they don't lose their life. They simply have to "pay" for the crime. In the spiritual sense, Christ already paid for our crimes, so we stand acquitted for past, present and future crimes (sins) against God. What Christ did, He did once, for all. So, while the Holy Spirit convicts us when we sin, He does not condemn us because we are in Christ and all our penalties have been paid and our eternal life is secure. Shout Hallelujah!!

Condemnation on the other hand is a death sentence. Using a courtroom setting, when someone is found guilty of a crime and is sentenced to death the judge states, "you are condemned to death by hanging until you are dead." "You are condemned to death by lethal injection, the gas chamber or the electric chair." See the difference. In the spiritual sense, the price of the crime of a lifetime of unrepentant sin is eternal death and damnation. Your life is condemned to hell for all eternity and in hell there is no life, only continual death.

In hell you are cut off from God, therefore you are cut off from anything Godly. There is no peace in hell, no hope, no compassion. There is no joy in hell, no friendship and no love. Hell is the place that is completely void of anything that is in the character of God.

In hell you will find dissention, hopelessness and anger. You'll find heart-ache, evil intentions and hatred. In hell you'll find everything that God is not because Satan is the exact oppose of God.

How many people do you know who want to spend their eternities in misery and pain? Cut off from anything good, anything kind, and anything truthful. People in hell will not be able to find rest for their minds or their hearts and they will be completely out of touch with their Creator. No one wants to live in this temporal life feeling unloved and unwanted, you certainly don't want to live out all eternity in those conditions.

So the next time you fall short and Satan starts to condemn you, you can say to him, "Satan, you are a liar. I cannot be condemned because I am in Christ, and in Christ there is no condemnation. My life, both now and forever more is secure and I will live and not die." Don't allow Satan to make you think he's telling you the truth. It's not in his makeup or character to ever tell the truth. Don't base how you feel about yourself or what you did on what Satan says, since you know he's a liar and the father of all lies. Don't think futile, think Christ-like. You can't be condemned, but because of God's great love for you, you will be convicted. But praise God because the penalties for your "crimes" against God were paid in full at Calvary. Whose report will you believe?

Grace and peace be unto you from God our Father and the Lord Jesus Christ.

If you are reading this chapter and can't say that you know that you've accepted Jesus Christ as your savior, why not do it now. You don't have to be in a church or have gotten your life in order; all you have to do is believe:

that Jesus is the only begotten Son of God
that He died for your sins

that God raised Jesus from the died, and
that Jesus is returning again.

If you believe these four things and you're ready
for Jesus to forgive your sins and position you live in
eternity with Him, humble your heart and say this
prayer:

"Heavenly Father, I know that I have
sinned against you and against your great
love for me, but as of right now I want to give
my life to you. I confess that I am a sinner
and that I need your forgiveness. I believe
that Jesus died to save me and I accept the
salvation that His life bought for me. For
give me Lord, wash away my sins and begin
the process of making me whole and
complete in you. I believe in my heart and
confess it with my mouth that Jesus is Lord
and as of right now, He is my Lord. Father,
thank you for my salvation and for the Holy
Spirit sealing me in you until the day Jesus
returns. I know my salvation is secured, no
matter how I feel or what I think, my
salvation is completely secure in Christ
Jesus. Thank you Lord, Amen."

Just like that my brother or sister, you are now
saved and in the Body of Christ. Hallelujah!!!

Whose Report – Part II

Our Personal Reports

Ephesians 4:17 "So I tell you this and insist on it in the Lord, that you must no longer live as the Gentiles do, in the futility of their thinking."

Ephesians 3:17 – 19 "...And I pray that you, being rooted and established in love may have power together with all the saints, to grasp how wide and long and high and deep is the love of Christ, and to know this love that surpasses knowledge that you maybe filled to the measure of all the fullness of God."

You know God wanted us to look at Satan's report, and after a close look we realize that Satan's report does not speak to us at all. But what are the other reports God is talking about? Well, much to my surprise the next report was the one we tell ourselves. This report is the most difficult for us to turn over to the word of God because we know ourselves. We know who we were, we know what we are and we may have an idea about who we want to be. We know our hopes, dreams and aspirations, but what we don't know is the full picture of who God has ordained us to be, which makes our report about ourselves faulty.

You see many of us have some things in our life that are not very complementary to our Christian walks. We know things we do and say that do not bode well for us as Christians. We know that we still have thoughts that are not Christ-like when we see men and women that we consider attractive. We know that there are still television shows that we shouldn't watch, videos we shouldn't rent, friends we shouldn't hang out with and vices we need to give up, but won't. So when God comes to us and tells us, "I want you to work with your hands on the thing(s) I've anointed you to do," we start giving our reports.

Report Number I - "I remember the last time I tried something like this I put myself in debt and it took me years to get out. I promised myself I'd never do that again. This couldn't be what God wants me to do. He knows what happened the last time."

Report Number 2 - "I would teach Sunday school, but I'm still a babe in Christ myself. I don't know enough to teach kids, even if there is a book I can use. I don't think I'm equipped to minister like that. What could God be thinking about asking me to help out in Education?"

Report Number 3 - "I know that I'm really good at putting together programs, I do it at work all day long and I always get wonderful evaluations. But church is just different. Somebody may say something about me. I just don't want to hear all that noise. Besides, God never leaves Himself short, He'll get someone else will do it if I don't."

Report Number 4 - "I really would like to help the music ministry. I've sung in a choir for years, I can play the piano a little and I could help direct, but I've got some ISSUES to work out before I can do anything. God will understand why I'm not doing what He told me to do."

Report Number 5 - "Oh, I just really hate being out front, Lord. I really just want to do something in the background. Yes, I know what you told me to do, but I don't want to do that."

Report Number 6 - "If I could take some of this weight off, change the color of my hair, get my nose fixed, let my children grow up (or any other excuse you can come up with,) I'd be ready to do the will of the Lord."

Our reports are always based on our past history, current knowledge or future dreams. Our reports are steeped in me, my and I and leave little to no room for God to work through us as He sees fit. Our reports usually include what others will think of us, what they will say about us or what we'll look like while we're doing what God told us to do. Very rarely are our reports based on *Jeremiah 1:5*, "Before I formed you in the womb I knew you, before you were born I set you apart. I appointed you as a prophet to the nations."

Nowhere in that scripture does God tell us that folks knew us before we were placed in the womb. Nowhere in that truth does it say we knew ourselves before God set us apart. Nowhere in that passage does it say that we have to like, understand or want to do what God set us apart to do. It only states, that from the very beginning, God had a plan for us and He knows what He set us apart to do.

Nowhere in that truth does it say that we had to be or have to be perfect or faultless.

The only thing God says is that He formed us, knew us and set us apart to become what He appointed us to become.

God knew we would not be perfect, but His report says, "I have appointed you." For Jeremiah, it was an appointment of prophecy, for me it is the appointment to proclaim the gospel in such a way that people can apply it to their lives, for you it may be to sing or write music, to be a scientist, an evangelist, a missionary, a doctor, a nurse, a dentist, or whatever God appointed you to be. God's report is always true for God is truth.

If your report about you doesn't include what God appointed you to be, and the knowledge that He can't tell a lie and therefore you can do what He's called you to do no matter what your past history shows, no matter what your current state of issues are and no matter what your future goals, objects and missions may be, your report is untrue. Whose report do you believe?

PRAYER:

Father, you created me in your image and in your likeness. I am perfected in you, able to accomplish all that you've said I can accomplish. I am made righteous in you, my old former life and ways have passed away and you have made my life anew. I am made to be your ambassador, to bring reconciliation to those who are lost and do not know you as Lord and Savior.

If I think less of myself than I ought to, please forgive me for treating myself as if I am less than a part of your royal priesthood.

Thank you Father for thinking enough of me to call me your child and to appointment to be more than a conquer through your son Christ Jesus, but you require my obedience. Help me be an obedient and mature son or daughter of the Most High God and help me to walk out the path you've carved out for me and not to be envious of other people's paths.

In Jesus name I pray. Amen.

Whose Report – Part III

The World's Report

Ephesians 4:17 "So I tell you this and insist on it in the Lord, that you must no longer live as the Gentiles do, in the futility of their thinking."

Ephesians 3:17 – 19 "...And I pray that you, being rooted and established in love may have power together with all the saints, to grasp how wide and long and high and deep is the love of Christ, and to know this love that surpasses knowledge that you maybe filled to the measure of all the fullness of God."

The world report is the next report. I usually read the Wall Street Journal every morning, follow the markets and see what companies are doing as far as profits and losses go. Most of the time it's just for fun and for education, but every once in a while I get angry with myself because I didn't buy a stock I had a chance to get when it was penny stock and now it's over $250.00 a share. Or the thought comes to mind that if I skipped paying my tithes for one month, I could buy several shares of a REAL investment stock, and then be able to pay even bigger tithes to God once the stock went up. I would be setting myself, my family and my church up for wealth, riches and fame, if I just didn't give that extra offering and put the money into an investment.

That's the world's thinking.

The world says that you can have this or you can't have that depending on how much money you have in the bank, what kind of job you have and what your credit looks like. The world says you don't give away anything, you barter with it, trade with it or you sell it, but if you give it away then you're being stupid and illogical because nothing is free.

The world says that if you don't have enough to meet your bills, you don't help someone else out who maybe worse off than you. The world says that you do other in before they can do you in, you hold on to and hoard everything you have because one day it maybe worth something and you don't want to think about how much money, wealth, fame or glory you missed out on because you gave something away that you really didn't need.

And the world says, if you want it, get it on credit. Charge anything you could possibly want and then pay if off monthly. Isn't that sweet? But the Word of God says something else. The Word of God says, pay your tithes and give your offerings and see if

God won't open up the windows of heaven and throw you out blessings you won't have room enough to receive. You need to understand something about that scripture. God can't throw anything out of the window until its open and the window won't be opened until you pay your tithes. But, the blessings are sitting behind the window, ready to be thrown if we'll just unlatch the window with our tithes and offerings and allow God to open up the windows, so that our ministering spirits, the angels, can reap the harvest that we've sown and get our blessings to us, (throwing them out of the windows of heaven, were there is an abundance of anything and everything we could possibly need, physical—healing for our bodies and minds; material—houses, cars, clothes and spiritual— gifts, revelation knowledge, etc.)

You see God has a very different financial plan than the world does. God's plan says, give. "Give and it will be given to you. A good measure, pressed down, shaken together and running over, will be poured into your lap. For with the measure you use, it will be measured to you," (*Luke 6:38.*)

Those who sow a lot of seed, reap a lot of harvest. Those who sow sparingly will reap sparingly. I sow big, because I want to reap big. My financial planner, God the Father Almighty, said that if sow good seed into good soil, I'll reap a big harvest. Nowhere in the Word of God does it say that I have to hoard clothes that I can't and haven't been able to wear in years. Nowhere in the Word of God does it say that I should sow my trust and faith into the world's soil and except to reap all the benefits of

God. No where in the Word of God does it say that I should put myself, wants, needs, desires and lust above what God has commanded me to do.

You have to sow into good soil and what better soil is there than the soil that furthers the gospel of Jesus Christ? Am I saying you should not invest? Of course not, but your trust, hope and faith is not in the investments. Your hope, faith, trust and belief rest solely on the Lord Jesus Christ, and you should listen to His report. When He tells you to give; give, to whom He tells you is in need. Give what He tells you to give them, and when He tells you to give it to them. No matter what our bank account may look like. No matter what needs you may have that have not been met, no matter what you had planned to do with the money, if He says give it, give it. And I can tell you the truth so that God may be glorified, YOU ARE BLESSED, and abundantly so. I'm a living witness.

If you believe God's financial report, you'll put away those credit cards too because they make you a bad steward of the monies God has given you authority over. Don't think so? Go home and look at the interest rate for all you credit cards. I'm sure you'll find some that are 12%, 15%, 18% even 22%. Paying all that extra money for something is a waste of God's resources. Think about it.

There's one last thing I want to leave you with. God does not care about how much money is in your bank account, what your credit looks like or anything else. If you believe His report and follow His plan you can ask for anything in His name and it shall be done. He will withhold no good thing from you. If God's told you, you can have a particular kind of car, house, boat, gift of the spirit or whatever your hearts desire is that He said you can have, go get it. Believe His report regarding your finances. Pay your tithes, give you offerings and reap your blessings.

PRAYER:

Lord, you have a plan for me that the world's system can't touch. In fact, the world and all its entrapments are passing away, but your Word will remain throughout eternity. Father, my finances are not where they should be. I'm in debt and I confess that I have not been the best steward of the money you've given me. Father, I've taken you for granite and ask for your forgiveness. I also ask that you begin to nurture me as I begin to take my responsibility to you, my church and my community serious. I know that I can't help those who maybe in need when I'm in need. My testimony has been tainted by my refusal to recognize that it is you who gives me strength to make wealth and that you give me wealth to cultivate things that are important to you, not to spend as I see fit. Change my mind and renew my heart, in Jesus name. Amen

Whose Report – Part IV
The God's Report

Ephesians 4:17 "So I tell you this and insist on it in the Lord, that you must no longer live as the Gentiles do, in the futility of their thinking."

Ephesians 3:17 – 19 "...And I pray that you, being rooted and established in love may have power together with all the saints, to grasp how wide and long and high and deep is the love of Christ, and to know this love that surpasses knowledge that you maybe filled to the measure of all the fullness of God."

The last report is the only one we should believe. It is the report of God about our lives; our obedience equals God's promises being fulfilled in our lives.

God clearly states over and over that He will bless us if we obey Him. In *Genesis 12:1 -2,* God is speaking to Abram and says "...leave your country, your people and your father's household and go to the land I will show you. I will make you a great nation and I will bless you. I will make your name great, and you will be blessed."

Abram was promised greatness in exchange for his trust in God. The Father asked Abram to go, but He didn't tell him where. The Lord told Abram to leave everything he knew—his home, his family, his friends and his traditions—and start a new life. God told Abram if you leave your inheritance I'll bless you with more than you currently have and the one thing you want more than anything else, children.

The promise of children came when God said "I will make you into a great nation." God was asking Abram to leave everything behind. Technically, God was asking Abram to leave his family unit and all ties that went along with his family behind. If that's the case, then how could Abram become a great nation without at least one child to carry on his name?

In *Genesis 15:2* Abram laments the fact that his estate is going to be left to a servant because he has no offspring. In order to make Abram a nation God had to give him and his wife an off spring. But the offspring didn't come for 25 years from the time God promised to the time Isaac was born. And with the birth of Isaac came the start of the great nation Abram had been promised.

The promise of blessings that God made Abram still hold true for children of God today. If we obey Him in all things, even when we don't understand and can't trace what he's doing, how he's doing it or the outcome of what it looks like he's doing, we still have to be obedient. God never says we have to understand, just that we have to obey.

God also promised that we'd have abundance if we obeyed and kept his commandments. In *Deuteronomy 28:1 – 14* the promise of Gods' blessings are laid out. *Deuteronomy 28:1 – 2* reads like this, "If you fully body the Lord your God and carefully follow all his commands I give you today, the Lord your God will set you high above the nations on earth. All these blessings will come upon you and accompany you if you obey the Lord your God," then, Moses lays out the blessings.

Remember, the Israelites were farmers and ranchers, so the things that were spoken of as being blessed for them made all the sense in the world at the time, but for us, we need to replace some of the elements that will be blessed with elements that are pertinent for us today. You can read this passage of scripture like this:

You will be blessed in the places where you feel safe and places where you don't.

Your children will be blessed.

The work you do on your job will be blessed.

Your cabinets, refrigerators and freezers will be blessed.

You will be blessed when you come into a situation and blessed when you leave the situation.

The Lord will allow your enemies at home, at school, at work or anywhere else, that rise up against you to be defeated in front of you and he will cause them to run from you as quickly as they can.

The Lord will send a blessing your bank accounts, your 401ks, your equities and investments.

The Lord will bless you right where you are.

The Lord will bless the work you do out of obedience with a supernatural blessing from heaven. You will be in a position to loan to others, but won't need a loan for yourself.

The Lord will make you come out first, with the best stuff, but you have to keep His commandments.

Conversely in verses *15 – 68 of Deuteronomy 28,* Moses points out what God will do if you don't obey His word. Suffice it to say you get the exact oppose of what God points out in verses 1-14. You won't be blessed in any way shape, form, or fashion if you deliberately and willfully disobey God.

Listening to any report other than God's is disobedience. Listening to Satan's, our own or the world's report puts us in a position of living our lives through lies because all the other reports leave God out of the equation.

Satan's report tells us lies about God and ourselves, just like he tricked Eve in the Garden of Eden by twisting the words of God, our enemy does the same thing today. Listening to him will leave us making plans and leaving God out because the enemy wants us to think we have the right to act independent of God, when in reality we can't do anything successfully without God. Anything done not in accordance with God's word is done without permission and outside of his purpose, which will leave us in the same position as Adam and Eve, out side the will of God and outside of his perfect plan for us.

Our report is predicated on our past history, failures and misfortunes. Our report also relies on our past victories and good fortunes, but if our report does not lead us to obey the word of God in general and the word of God specifically for us, then we'll find that we're like David. We may be appointed and anointed by God for a specific task but we're not in a position to fulfill our call because we've chosen to do things our way and not God's way.

When David saw Bathsheba he was in the wrong place at the wrong time, (*II Samuel 11*.) As the king he should have been in battle with his troops, not at home in his castle. Not being where he should have been cost David dearly. It cost him his integrity—he killed an innocent man in order to cover up his sin, (*II Samuel 11:14 – 17*.) It caused a rife in his relationship with God—when the prophet Nathan went to David and confronted him about his affair with Bathsheba and his murder of her husband Uriah, David had to repent, (*II Samuel 12:1 – 13a,*) and he lost his offspring—a portion of his future, (*II Samuel 12:15 – 19*.)

Even though David was a man after God's heart, he still sinned and fell short of the glory of God because he listened to his own report. He did not put God in the decision making process when he was thinking about what he wanted to do with Bathsheba and he husband. If he had, he would have been on the battle field and not walking on the roof top of his castle and none of the following events would have taken place.

Abraham and Sarah sinned when Sarah concocted the plan to give Hagar to Abram for the purpose of having a child. Abraham was just as wrong as Sarah because he gave in to her request over what he knew God had commanded.

But, Abraham, Sarah and David, despite their sinning against God, found out that God is not a man that he should lie or the son of man that he should change his mind, (*Numbers 23:19.*) God made all of them promises, which He kept regardless of their actions.

God is a covenant making, covenant enabling and covenant keeping God. He never goes back on His word. He's promises are true and have their yes in Christ Jesus. Nothing we could ever do would cause God to turn His back on His word. He has exalted His word above everything and His name above His word. According to *John 1:14* the word became flesh and dwelled among men. The word the John is speaking of is Jesus.

God promised a Messiah and He sent Jesus. God promised a savior and He sent Jesus. He promised that He would give us live and that live would be in abundance. He sent Jesus to be our example, to show us how to live above mediocrity and how to live our lives completely surrendered to God.

God's report speaks to us from a place that no one can really know. God's report speaks to us out of his unfathomable love for us—an unfathomable love for all mankind.

From Adam and Eve to today mankind has consistently lacked trust and faith in God and has failed to be obedient, but God has loved us anyway. Even as Christians, we often seek our own ways ignoring or neglecting the teachings that God has left for us, but God loves us anyway. How could a holy God love, so deeply and absolutely and unholy people? Because God is love, (*I John 4:8, 16.*)

The love of God is not a part of His character, it is the sum total of who God is and the other traits of his character stem from His great love. God's long-suffering, compassion, mercy, grace, kindness, tenderness and all other qualities and attributes that can be extolled upon Him all come from His love for mankind, the crowning jewel of His creation. That's why God wants to bless us, because he loves us. He wants us to have everything we need and not to lack anything.

And all God ask in return for giving us such a great unsearchable love is our obedience.

God's report is true, right and inerrant. The same can not be said for Satan's report, the world's report or our reports. Which report will you believe? Which report will you follow?

If you have never accepted Jesus Christ as Savior, but you realize that you need to change whose report you're listening to and living through, I invite you to pray this simple prayer.

PRAYER:

Father God, I thank you for loving me so much. I appreciate your thinking about me, caring about me and positioning me as the apple of your eye. I come to you to ask for forgiveness of my sins, both known and unknown and I confess that I am a sinner in need of Christ Jesus the Savior, the only Son of God. Come into my heart and make me yours completely. I believe that my salvation is done and secured in Christ Jesus. In Jesus name I pray and give thanks to God, amen.

Printed in the United States
40876LVS00002B/55-102

9 781413 792195